Cultural Studies

Theorizing Politics, Politicizing Theory

VOLUME 16 NUMBER 4 JULY 2002

Special Issue
Who Needs Cultural Intermediaries?

Edited by
Sean Nixon and Paul Du Gay

Editorial Statement

Cultural Studies continues to expand and flourish, in large part because the field keeps changing. Cultural studies scholars are addressing new questions and discourses, continuing to debate long-standing issues, and reinventing critical traditions. More and more universities have some formal cultural studies presence; the number of books and journals in the field is rapidly increasing. *Cultural Studies* welcomes these developments. We understand the expansion, reflexivity and internal critique of cultural studies to be both signs of its vitality and signature components of its status as a field. At the same time, cultural studies has been – and will no doubt continue to be – the subject of numerous attacks, launched from various perspectives and sites. These have to be taken seriously and answered, intellectually, institutionally and publicly. *Cultural Studies* hopes to provide a forum for response and strategic discussion.

    Cultural Studies assumes that the knowledge formations that make up the field are as historically and geographically contingent as are the determinations of any cultural practice or configuration and that the work produced within or at its permeable boundaries will be diverse. We hope not only to represent but to enhance this diversity. Consequently, we encourage submissions from various disciplinary, theoretical and geographical perspectives, and hope to reflect the wide-ranging articulations, both global and local, among historical, political, economic, cultural and everyday discourses. At the heart of these articulations are questions of community, identity, agency and change.

    We expect to publish work that is politically and strategically driven, empirically grounded, theoretically sophisticated, contextually defined and reflexive about its status, however critical, within the range of cultural studies. *Cultural Studies* is about theorizing politics and politicizing theory. How this is to be accomplished in any context remains, however, open to rigorous enquiry. As we look towards the future of the field and the journal, it is this enquiry that we especially hope to support.

Lawrence Grossberg
Della Pollock   *January 1998*

Contributions should be sent to Professors Lawrence Grossberg and Della Pollock, Dept. of Communication Studies, CB #3285, 113 Bingham Hall, The University of North Carolina at Chapel Hill, Chapel Hill, NC 27599-3285, USA. They should be in triplicate and should conform to the reference system set out in the Notes for Contributors. An abstract of up to 300 words (including 6 key-words) should be included for purposes of review. Submissions undergo blind peer review. Therefore, the author's name, address and e-mail should appear *only* on a detachable cover page and not anywhere else on the manuscript. Every effort will be made to complete the review process within six months of submission. A disk version of the manuscript must be provided in the appropriate software format upon acceptance for publication.

Reviews, and books for review, should be sent to Tim O'Sullivan, School of Arts, de Montfort University, The Gateway, Leicester LE1 9BH; or to Graeme Turner, Deptartment of English, University of Queensland, Brisbane, Queensland 4072, Australia; or to Gil Rodman, Department of Communication, University of South Florida, 4202 East Fowler Avenue, CIS 1040, Tampa, FL 33620-7800, USA.

Contents

VOLUME 16   NUMBER 4   JULY 2002

Articles

Sean Nixon and Paul du Gay
WHO NEEDS CULTURAL INTERMEDIARIES?   **495**

Keith Negus
THE WORK OF CULTURAL INTERMEDIARIES AND THE
ENDURING DISTANCE BETWEEN PRODUCTION AND
CONSUMPTION   **501**

Angela McRobbie
CLUBS TO COMPANIES: NOTES ON THE DECLINE OF POLITICAL
CULTURE IN SPEEDED UP CREATIVE WORLDS   **516**

Liz McFall
WHAT ABOUT THE OLD CULTURAL INTERMEDIARIES?
AN HISTORICAL REVIEW OF ADVERTISING PRODUCERS   **532**

Lise Skov
HONG KONG FASHION DESIGNERS AS CULTURAL
INTERMEDIARIES: OUT OF GLOBAL GARMENT PRODUCTION   **553**

Matthew Soar
THE FIRST THINGS FIRST MANIFESTO AND THE POLITICS OF
CULTURAL JAMMING: TOWARDS A CULTURAL ECONOMY OF
GRAPHIC DESIGN AND ADVERTISING   **570**

Book review

Catherine Johnson
WORKING THROUGH TELEVISION   **593**

Notes on contributors   **596**

Note of thanks   **597**

Notes for contributors   **598**

Routledge
Taylor & Francis Group

Sean Nixon and Paul du Gay

WHO NEEDS CULTURAL INTERME-DIARIES?

IN DOUGLAS ADAMS' comic science fiction saga *The Hitchhiker's Guide to the Galaxy* (BBC Radio Four, 1978; and BBC TV, 1981), Arthur Dent, the tale's hapless hero, finds himself stranded towards the end of his epic adventure on a huge transporter space ship – an 'ark' – carrying a dormant human population towards a new brighter future on some unspecified planet. Dent and his companion, Ford Prefect, are puzzled by the odd array of social types residing within the ark; second-hand car salesmen, advertising account executives, television producers, insurance salesmen, personnel officers, public relations executives and management consultants. When they question the craft's ineffectual captain about this odd collection of types, he reveals that they are on the 'B' ark, one of three launched from the planet of Golgafrincham because of fears that a great catastrophe was about to engulf the world. The captain explains that into the 'A' ark went all the 'brilliant leaders, the scientists, the great artists, all the achievers', while into the 'C' ship went all the people who 'do the actual work, who make things and do things'. The 'B' ark contained, as they had discovered, the 'middle men'. As the travellers pursue their questioning, it transpires that the 'B' ark's unlikely human cargo have, in fact, been duped into embarking on their voyage and that the remaining population of Golgafrincham have never left their home planet. The tale of impending doom had been a spurious one concocted by the productive social groups of Golgafrincham in order to rid themselves of the 'useless third of the population'. By means of this ruse, the Golgafrinchams had managed to create a world free from the unwarranted attention of management consultants, PR executives and advertising account executives and gone on to live full and prosperous lives.

Douglas Adams' satire upon the 'useless' middling sorts of Golgafrincham and its nightmare vision of a society entirely populated by the likes of management consultants and PR people (the society of the 'B' ark), belongs within a well established genre of writings about, and denigrations of, middling social groups

Cultural Studies ISSN 0950-2386 print/ISSN 1466-4348 online © 2002 Taylor & Francis Ltd
http://www.tandf.co.uk/journals
DOI: 10.1080/09502380210139070

– particularly the lower middle classes. As Geoff Crossick and Heinz-Gerhard
Haupt have noted, a whole genre of literary condescension from Balzac and Zola
to H. G. Wells and Brecht has attacked the social and political standing of this
social stratum (Crossick and Haupt, 1995: 1). Often these critiques were notable
for not only their venom, but also for being written by individuals moving away
from their own petite bourgeois backgrounds. As Peter Bailey demonstrates,
British post-war writers like John Osborne (the son of an advertising man)
offered self-mocking accounts of a social stratum that they knew from the inside
and from which they were social migrants (Bailey, 1999). And it is significant that
in taking to task the 'unproductive middling groups', Douglas Adams was also
turning on a social fraction close to his own subaltern origins (Adams was the
son of a teacher and a nurse). The occupational groups that figure in Adams'
satire are noteworthy in other ways, though. They represent (second-hand car
salesmen notwithstanding) those parts of the lower middle class that have caught
the eye of a range of social commentators over recent years. Advertising practitioners, management consultants, PR people, and so on, belong to those intermediary occupations involving information and knowledge intensive forms of
work that have come to be seen as increasingly central to economic and cultural
life (this is, of course, the point of Adams satire). In this Special Issue of *Cultural
Studies* we turn to these occupational groups and to the conceptual terminology
that has been mobilized both to place them in the occupational division of labour
and understand the social roles they perform. At the heart of this is the idea of
'cultural intermediaries'.

The term 'cultural intermediaries' – or, more precisely, 'new cultural intermediaries' – is most associated with Pierre Bourdieu and is used by him to
describe groups of workers involved in the provision of symbolic goods and
services. Bourdieu's most extended reference to this group of workers comes in
his discussion of middle-brow culture in his mammoth book, *Distinction*
(Bourdieu, 1984), where he identifies 'the producers of cultural programmes on
television or radio or the critics of "quality" newspapers and magazines and all
the writer-journalists and journalist-writers' as 'the most typical' of this group
(Bourdieu, 1984: 315). Elsewhere he includes practitioners in design, packaging, sales promotion, PR, marketing and advertising within the category of 'new
cultural intermediaries', and also cites the example of those involved in the provision of medical and social assistance (such as marriage guidance counselors, sex
therapists and dieticians).

As this list of occupations suggests, Bourdieu's notion of 'new cultural intermediaries' is an inclusive, if not quite a catchall, category. He clearly mobilizes
the term to capture shifts in the occupational structure in France (and by impli-
cation other Western societies) since the 1960s that have seen the growth of
educated and salaried occupations in both the public and private sector. These
are shifts that other writers – such as Lash and Urry – have described as marking
the emergence of a new 'service class' (Lash and Urry, 1987), whilst the terms

'new middle class' and 'new petite bourgeoisie' have also been mobilized to capture these changes in the social structure that have undeniably seen an expansion of the 'social middle' or what was more typically referred to in nineteenth century France as the 'classes moyennes' (Crossick and Haupt, 1995; Burns, 1986).

Bourdieu most strongly links the expansion of this group of 'new cultural intermediaries' and their increasing salience in the occupational structure to the bourgeoning of the consumer sectors of the economy and the associated consolidation of large broadcasting and media organizations. In fact, he sees the new cultural intermediaries as germane to the 'ethical retooling' of consumer capitalism and its promotion of a 'morality of pleasure as duty' (Bourdieu, 1984: 365–71). Bound up with their new prominence is an assertion from Bourdieu that these groups of workers are able to exert, from their position within the cultural institutions, a certain amount of cultural authority as shapers of taste and the inculcators of new consumerist dispositions. Significantly, this is an authority that brings them into conflict with what Bourdieu calls the legitimate producers and reproducers – what we might call traditional intellectuals. And the tension between 'traditional' and 'new intellectuals' is an important, if underdeveloped, theme in Bourdieu's comments on the 'new cultural intermediaries'.

In picking up on Bourdieu's lead, there is still plenty of work to do in both conceptualizing and substantively exploring the position and status of cultural intermediaries. Here we want to offer a few pointers in order to frame the articles that follow in this special issue. The first of these concerns the problematic qualifier 'new' that Bourdieu attaches to 'cultural intermediaries' in *Distinction*. This throws up the question of periodization in relation to the apparent expansion in cultural intermediary occupations. If you like, how new are these occupations and when did they expand? Certainly, the evidence from Britain suggests the need for caution in talking uncritically about the expansion of cultural intermediaries and assigning to them the epithet 'new'. Occupations such as broadcasting and advertising, alongside journalism, expanded markedly in the first half of the twentieth century and, in the case of advertising, decline in terms of the number of people employed from a high point of the 1960s. In no sense, then, are these occupations particularly new and nor are they necessarily expanding (though for a counter argument about the increase in the numbers employed in 'creative work' see Scase and Davis, 1999). There is a need, then, to separate the question of the quantitative expansion of cultural intermediaries from their apparent increasing salience and influence over economic and cultural life. The latter may occur, despite the relative numerical decline of these sectors. This is why we prefer to talk about 'cultural intermediaries', rather than 'new cultural intermediaries'.

Secondly, as we have already suggested, Bourdieu's notion of new cultural intermediaries – and the way the term has been taken up by other writers – is very inclusive and this poses some problems. The most serious concerns the way the term tends to cut across distinct occupational formations, cultures and forms of expertise, as well as the rather different social composition of discrete cultural intermediary occupations. Thus, for example, broadcasters, journalists and producers in Britain – most especially in the BBC – are a very different occupational formation in terms of social and educational backgrounds and occupational ethos from, say, advertising creatives (Burns, 1977; Nixon, forthcoming). A more differentiated account of these occupations is therefore required; one that can grasp the differences between them, as much as 'family resemblances'.

Thirdly, and following on from the previous two points, there is a serious need for more substantive work on cultural intermediary occupations in order to empirically ground claims about both their place in the occupational structure and the role they play in economic and cultural life. This is particularly important given that quite large claims are made about the significance of these occupational groups – notably by Bourdieu and Featherstone – without much being known about them. Featherstone (1991), for example, cites no empirical evidence about occupations he sees as central to cultural change. At issue here is also the need to disentangle the study of cultural intermediaries from the excessive value judgments that have dogged assessments of these groups. Commentators have either denigrated them, as Bourdieu does, as the source of new forms of social conservatism (and Bourdieu's analysis is notable for its intemperate tone and falls into that genre of antipathy towards the lower middle classes with which we begin) or else celebrated them for their links to a progressive, post-'68 counter culture (as Featherstone does). What we suggest is needed is a more sober assessment of these groups which avoids the pitfalls of either celebration or denunciation.

Finally, and perhaps most importantly, we want to suggest that there is considerable strategic value to be gained from focusing upon these intermediary occupations. They force, on the one hand, an opening up of the arena of cultural circulation, which has been poorly studied within cultural studies. In particular, in relation to the study of the commercial domain and commercially produced culture, they shift our attention away from the over-emphasis on the moment of consumption that has tended to dominate recent accounts of the commercial field. In doing so, they open up the links between production and consumption and the interplay between these discrete moments in the lifecycle of cultural forms. More than that, by focusing on both the formal expertise and broader intellectual and cultural formation of these practitioners, it becomes possible to scrutinize the links between economic and cultural practices within the sphere of commercial cultural production; a scrutiny that can bring to light, as we have argued elsewhere, the interdependence and relations of reciprocal effect between cultural and economic practices (Nixon, 1996; du Gay, 1997).

The contributors to this volume each, in their different ways, pick up on these conceptual provocations raised by the concept of cultural intermediaries. Keith Negus and Liz McFall both emphasize the need to qualify the conceptual reach of the term and to contest some of the more ambitious claims made in its name. For Negus, amongst other things, there is a need to relativize the emphasis on the more 'creative' kinds of intermediary occupations by looking at the more prosaic, but crucial contributions of practitioners like accountants working within cultural institutions. For McFall, the study of cultural intermediaries requires careful historical qualification. And while they both continue to deploy the term, they each offer important revisions. Liz McFall's article further demonstrates the value of sustained empirical reflection on this grouping of workers and she brings a quizzical eye and historical sensitivity to that most neophiliac and presentist of occupations, advertising. Lise Skov and Matt Soar's respective papers also add much to our knowledge of discrete cultural intermediary occupations. What emerges from their papers is a clearer sense (in Soar's case) of both the professional ideologies of advertising and design practitioners and (in Skov's case) the particular conditions under which fashion designers labour.

Angela McRobbie also centrally addresses the characteristics of work within these occupations. Focusing on contemporary public debates in Britain about the 'creative industries', she offers a bold sense of a number of contradictory dynamics at work in this sector. These include both the heady celebration of 'fun at work' in these occupations and the high levels of insecurity and individualism that mark out their employment relations. Engaging with contemporary sociological accounts about reflexive modernization and the growth of what Zygmunt Bauman has called the 'individualized society', McRobbie further ponders on whether these areas of work pose in a particularly sharp way processes of re-traditionalization within economic life. For McRobbie, like the other contributors, it is the capacity of cultural intermediaries to condense and focus broader questions about social and cultural change which makes them worthy of study and why cultural intermediaries do, in this sense, matter.

References

Adams, Douglas (1978) *The Hitchhiker's Guide to the Galaxy*. BBC Radio Four.

Adams, Douglas (1981) *The Hitchhiker's Guide to the Galaxy*. BBC Television.

Bailey, Peter (1999) 'White collars, grey lives? The lower middle class revisited'. *The Journal of British Studies*, 38: 273–90.

Bourdieu, Pierre (1984) [1979] *Distinction, a Social Critique of the Judgement of Taste*. London: Routledge.

Burns, Tom (1977) *The BBC: Public Institution and Private World*. London: Macmillan.

Burns, Val (1986) 'The discovery of the new middle class'. *Theory & Society*, 15(3): 345.

Crossick, Geoffrey and Haupt, Heinz-Gerhard (1995) *The Petite Bourgeoisie in Europe 1780–1914, Enterprise, Family and Independence*. London & New York: Routledge.

Du Gay, Paul (1997) 'Introduction'. In P. Du Gay (ed.) *Production of Culture / Cultures of Production*. London: Sage, pp. 1–10.

Featherstone, Mike (1991) *Postmodernism and Consumer Culture*. London: Sage.

Nixon, Sean (1996) *Hard Looks, Masculinities, Spectatorship and Contemporary Consumption*. London and New York: UCL Press & St. Martin's Press.

Nixon, Sean (forthcoming) *Creative Cultures, Gender and Creativity at Work in Advertising*. London: Sage.

Scase, Richard and Davis, Howard (2000) *Managing Creativity, the Dynamics of Work and Organization*. Milton Keynes: Open University Press.

CULTURAL STUDIES 16(4) 2002, 501–515

Routledge
Taylor & Francis Group

Keith Negus

THE WORK OF CULTURAL INTER-MEDIARIES AND THE ENDURING DISTANCE BETWEEN PRODUCTION AND CONSUMPTION

Abstract

This article raises some critical questions about cultural intermediaries as both a descriptive label and analytic concept. In doing so, it has two main aims. First, it seeks to provide some clarification, critique and suggestions that will assist in the elaboration of this idea and offer possible lines of enquiry for further research. Second, it is argued that whilst studying the work of cultural intermediaries can provide a number of insights, such an approach provides only a partial account of the practices that continue to proliferate in the space between production and consumption. Indeed, in significant ways, a focus on cultural intermediaries reproduces rather than bridges the distance between production and consumption. The paper focuses on three distinct issues. First, some questions are raised about the presumed special significance of cultural intermediaries within the production/consumption relations of contemporary capitalism. Second, how 'creative' and active cultural intermediaries are within processes of cultural production is discussed. Third, specific strategies of inclusion/exclusion adopted by this occupational grouping are highlighted in order to suggest that access to work providing 'symbolic goods and services' is by no means as fluid or open as is sometimes claimed.

Keywords

cultural intermediaries; culture industries; Bourdieu; work

Cultural Studies ISSN 0950-2386 print/ISSN 1466-4348 online © 2002 Taylor & Francis Ltd
http://www.tandf.co.uk/journals
DOI: 10.1080/09502380210139089

THE TERM CULTURAL intermediaries has become increasingly used in recent years, often in a manner that bears little resemblance to its introduction in the writings of Pierre Bourdieu, and its adoption by those who draw on this aspect of his work. The term can be found used in a precise way, but also in a quite casual manner. With this in mind, I want to use this essay to offer both some clarification and to raise some critical questions about the notion of cultural intermediaries. I want to suggest that the significance this label accords to an occupational group and set of working practices is warranted due to the way it directs attention to significant changes brought about by the growth of workers involved in the production and circulation of symbolic forms, and because a focus on this type of employment highlights some of the central dilemmas of how to deal with the articulations of production and consumption. As a theoretical analytic category and as a descriptive label for an occupational entity, the notion of new cultural intermediaries provides a number of insights and points to some important lines of enquiry. However, we still have a long way to go before we come close to fully understanding the practices that continue to proliferate in the space between production and consumption, particularly in those gaps opened up by the media, arts, information and entertainment industries. In focusing on debates about the practices that involve the intersection and possible blurring of production/consumption, one of my aims here is to highlight the enduring significance of the *distance* between production and consumption.

There are three distinct areas I wish to focus on. First, I want to address a question that seems obvious, but leads into a number of problems: who are cultural intermediaries and what is their special position in the relations of production/consumption? I then move on to my second question, which concerns how 'creative' and active cultural intermediaries are within processes of cultural production. Third, I want to ask about the strategies of inclusion/exclusion adopted by this occupational grouping.

Cultural intermediaries as a special occupational grouping linking production to consumption

The term 'cultural intermediaries' was introduced by Pierre Bourdieu in his book *Distinction* and was associated with his comments on the 'new petite bourgeoisie', a new faction of middle-class workers that has grown in size and influence since the middle of the twentieth century. Although Bourdieu's ideas are derived from detailed studies of work and consumption in France, the concept has certain similarities with what other writers have called a 'service class' or 'knowledge class'. It refers to those workers engaged in 'occupations involving presentation and representation . . . providing symbolic goods and services' (Bourdieu, 1984: 359). To repeat a much cited passage:

> The new petite bourgeoisie comes into its own in all the occupations involving presentation and representation (sales, marketing, advertising, public relations, fashion, decoration and so forth) and in all the institutions providing symbolic goods and services . . . and in cultural production and organization which have expanded considerably in recent years. (1984: 359)

This new petite bourgeoisie distinguish themselves from the old petite bourgeoisie (with its middle brow dispositions) and adopt different orienting practices towards their own 'class' identity. In both their working habits and routines of daily living, this new class faction tends to blur a number of conventional distinctions. Most notable here is the division between high art/popular culture, and the divide between personal taste and professional judgement (or leisure and work). This blurring can be observed in the practices of workers in the media, arts and entertainment industries, and particularly in advertising and marketing, occupations that have become central to the workings of capitalism in general. According to Bourdieu – and also to Mike Featherstone (1991) who adopts the term in his account of postmodern consumer culture – this new class faction implies a certain meeting or point of connection between the disaffected, educated, bohemian middle class and the upwardly mobile, newly educated working class (it is not difficult to see why this grouping might have an appeal for those engaged in doing media and cultural studies).

Bourdieu does not expand on his analysis of this group in any detailed way, and it is rather surprising that there is no real sense of the work of cultural intermediaries in his studies of artistic and literary production (Bourdieu, 1993, 1996). Although focused on nineteenth- and early twentieth-century aesthetic fields, we might have expected to find more detailed references to the emergent groupings and practices that would more widely be recognized as cultural intermediary activity in the latter part of the twentieth century. It has mainly been down to other researchers to begin developing, elaborating or illustrating this idea through empirical research. Here I would include my own work on the music industry in the UK (Negus, 1992), and the USA (Negus, 1999), and in light of this I would like to briefly say something about the value of this notion and why I have used it.

The central strength of the notion of cultural intermediaries is that it places an emphasis on those workers who come *in-between* creative artists and consumers (or, more generally, production and consumption). It also suggests a shift away from unidirectional or transmission models of cultural production towards an approach that conceives of workers as intermediaries continually engaged in forming a point of connection or articulation between production and consumption. This is a significant shift from transmission models of cultural production whereby various writers have portrayed the aesthetic economy in terms of analogies with assembly lines, or 'filter flow' systems, tracing the movement of 'raw materials' from creative artist to consumer (see Hirsch, 1972; Peterson, 1976; Ryan and Peterson, 1982).

It also suggests a shift from, or counterbalance to, an emphasis on economic constraints and determinations (from the economic shaping of culture), associated with versions of political economy, towards a concern with how culture shapes the economic. Or, more precisely and in less causal terms, it challenges us to think about the reciprocal inter-relationship of what are often thought of as discrete 'cultural' and 'economic' practices. Hence, Bourdieu's work is pivotal in the resurrection of or return to a 'cultural economy' of social life.

Bourdieu, and those who draw on this aspect of his work, suggests that symbolic production is central to the work of cultural intermediaries, and this frequently means the use of advertising imagery, marketing and promotional techniques. Such symbolic productions are crucial for contemporary commodification to occur. Hence, cultural intermediaries shape both use values and exchange values, and seek to manage how these values are connected with people's lives through the various techniques of persuasion and marketing and through the construction of markets. The aim of numerous workers engaged in promotion and marketing is to link a product to a potential consumer by seeking to forge a sense of identification, whether between a young person and a training shoe, a spectator and a film star, or a listener and a musician. Here, the use of advertising imagery, marketing and promotion are central to the representations through which attempts are made to link a product, service or celebrity and a citizen. As new products, celebrities and services are created, so cultural intermediaries become continually involved in explaining to us the use value of these new commodities (why we might need and what we might do with new face creams, training shoes, bendy curved toothbrushes, or young classical singers) and what their exchange value might be (their relative market worth). Hence, the study of cultural intermediaries should provide important insights into the changing dynamics of contemporary capitalism.

However, this approach to these issues creates a number of problems. The concept of cultural intermediaries has been introduced in a way that privileges a particular cluster of occupations. It accords certain workers a pivotal role in these processes of symbolic mediation, prioritizing a narrow and reductionist aesthetic definition of culture (and, despite various gestures, seeming to forget the insights of many years of anthropology and sociology). Hence, representation, 'meaning' and the symbolic are treated as 'cultural', whereas the notion of culture as a 'whole way of life' seems to be rather marginalized or forgotten – or applied only to the selected workers engaged in 'symbolic' activities. So, advertising executives, designers and magazine journalists are cultural intermediaries, whereas it seems that biologists, physicists, accountants, priests and trade union leaders are not. Yet there are many other occupational groupings that are crucial to processes of cultural mediation or the linkages which might connect consumption with production. Indeed, a consideration of who might bridge this space, or who might be involved in 'articulating' production with consumption, raises some significant questions about the enduring *distance* between production and consumption.

I want to develop this point further by focusing on two groupings of workers engaged in many of the symbolic practices attributed to 'cultural intermediaries', but who do not perhaps occupy the type of petite bourgeoisie 'class position' implied by Bourdieuian notions of cultural intermediaries. The first group is comprised of senior managers or senior corporate executives, business analysts and accountants – the people who are often routinely referred to as 'the suits' (in the music business, Hollywood and the advertising industry), a term that is in many ways a romantic conceit that is deployed rhetorically within such industries during various classification struggles and as a means by which the so-called 'creatives' attempt to establish their distance from the demands of budgets and financial constraints ('the suit' being the index of such constraints). Accountants are key intermediaries who are called upon to deploy their given expertise at moments when uncertainty (or risk) is pervasive; when senior executives (in the music or film industry) are unclear how to judge the creative abilities of the staff they have appointed; when corporations need to assess their portfolio of artistic assets (whether books, authors, musicians, recordings, etc.); or when a company involved in cultural production is assessing their attempts to construct or imagine the public as a market.

Accounting knowledge has emerged as a particular way of ordering and assessing the actions of individuals within multi-divisional corporations. It provides a way of privileging 'hard' data (facts, figures, statistics) over 'soft' explanations (human foibles, intuitive hunches and 'belief in an artist'). Yet, the procedures of accounting are by no means as objective, straightforward or guided by rational 'economic' calculation, as is sometimes assumed. Geert Hofstede, following his experience of working in various industries and from years of research, reached the conclusion that accounting systems are little more than 'uncertainty-reducing rituals'. Accountants fulfil 'a cultural need for certainty, simplicity and truth in a confusing world, regardless of whether this truth has any objective base' (Hofstede, 1991: 151). Certain actions are reduced to figures and these are then abstracted out of the social context within which they were created and which they seek to explain. Hofstede argues that corporate budget practices are often little more than a 'game', driven less by any clear financial logic than an attempt to maintain morale in the face of uncertainty.

There is a considerable body of work, itself owing a debt to the writings of Max Weber, which suggests that accounting knowledge is grounded in very specific spatial and historical circumstances and which points to the way that accountants continually produce changing symbolic representations that are historically specific (see Jones, 1995). In addition, accountants do not simply 'account' in some instrumental way anymore than talent scouts solely assess 'talent' without any consideration for budgets, the commercial 'market' or financial matters. The significance of accountants and business affairs staff is severely down played if they are simply reduced to 'suits' and assumed to have little understanding of and contribution towards the creative process. Whilst the high powered executives and star artists may continually move between the few major entertainment corporations and whilst a continual stream of young staff may come and go, financial analysts, legal staff and accountants can remain with the same corporation for many years and provide a source of stability, often remaining with a company for years and enduring changing fashions, the rise and fall of different star personas, and corporate take-overs and mergers.

To give an example from my own work on the music industry, it is usually artist and repertoire (A & R) staff who are thought of as the initial point of contact for any new artist who may be signing to a company. Yet it is the business affairs people (accountants and lawyers) who will be involved in drawing up the finer details of any contract and negotiating with performers and their representatives. A & R staff may provide a hip face, may hang out in the mythical 'street' and club, may discuss song arrangements with their artists and book an act into a studio. But it is business affairs staff who will approve the payments to the studio. If a band find themselves recording on a Sunday morning and suddenly decide that they require additional equipment or session musicians and that this will take them over budget, then it is more usually the signature of the head of business affairs that will release the funds to allow the creative process to continue. Hence, an artist's personal relationship with the director of business affairs is arguably more important than their repartee with the young scout who may have first seen them playing in a club and who may be with a competing company or working in a record shop in two years time. Business affairs staff assess the economic potential of any acquisition over both short and long term. They are then involved in continually monitoring an artist's economic performance and will judge at which point a performer, catalogue or genre is no longer commercially viable. This is not simply a 'financial' decision but impacts upon the symbolic production of the company's repertoire, not only in terms of who is selected to remain at the company, but also due to the subtle ways in which the musical preferences of the president of business affairs, and the nature of his or her personal relations with artists, can influence the judgements made.

Hence, it is important to incorporate the work and dispositions of accountants into an understanding of the activities of cultural intermediaries. These workers do not simply represent the financial pressures of 'commerce' (counterposed against art or creativity). They are involved in the construction of what is to be 'commercial' at any one time, often retrospectively, and they are engaged in mediating many of the values through which aesthetic work is realized (Negus, 1995, 1998). If we are to understand the more general relations between production and consumption, then we need to understand the symbolic, and the cultural in the broadest sense of the term, as well as the narrowly economic practices of business analysts and accountants. We should also think about the ties that bind 'cultural intermediaries' firmly into these established institutionalized structures of production.

One such connection can be highlighted by considering the work of a well established occupational group with a direct relationship to 'cultural intermediaries' – workers in a factory. The activities that take place in the manufacturing plant or assembly line may be less apparent than the cultural service work of editors, journalists and designers, due to the geographical location (and relocation) of factories and warehouses to parts of the country, city or world where labour is cheaper or concealed. In numerous industries involved in cultural production, the work of the so-called 'creatives' is often far removed from the manufacturing process. This is an issue that is highlighted by Angela McRobbie (1998) in her work on the fashion industry, where she observes that fashion students tend not to visit factories and production units. Designers often have little knowledge of who makes up their clothes, how much they are paid and where it is done. The 'creative' impulse breeds a certain distaste for, denial of and even contempt for the day-to-day realities of manufacturing labour and warehouse work. Cultural intermediaries are in significant ways prone to encourage the establishment of a distance between themselves and industrial manufacturing, storage and shipment of the symbolic items that they have a stake in 'mediating'.

In a similar way, those who are apparently being encouraged to get ever closer to consumers – personnel working in retail (du Gay, 1996) – are often equally unaware of the biographies of the products they are selling on a daily basis. This can be as true of the latest fashionable training shoes or dresses, electronic components or coffee beans, which may all be extracted from sweated and impoverished labourers, as it is of the artisanal, 'traditional' crafts produced by peasants. As Nestor Garcia Canclini (1982, 1993) found in his research on 'popular cultures' within capitalism in Mexico, those employed in stores and boutiques selling 'traditional' crafts often had no idea where the articles they were selling had come from. They had no knowledge of who had produced them, nor were they aware of the original purpose of such artifacts (they had simply become 'authentic' folk souvenirs for tourists). In part, this situation had come about as a direct consequence of the activities of a group of workers whom Garcia Canclini identifies as 'intermediaries' linking the town to the remote village, connecting the peasant farmer to the urban entrepreneur, and who were engaged in integrating a 'traditional' form of production into the commodity system and modern capitalist relations of market exchange.

Some studies have shown that the cultural intermediaries of marketing and public relations can play a critical role in connecting production to consumption in such a way that their practices can shape the product and, in some significant way, feed the practices of the public back into the design and marketing process as a form of social knowledge (du Gay et al., 1997). But this is not always the case. Far more frequently, there is no enduring 'articulation' nor substantive dynamic linking production with consumption. Instead, there are fleeting

moments of contact as products are passed from workers aligned more according to Jean Paul Sartre's (1976) notion of series, relating to each other through
the most habitual and superficial of unreflexive transactions conducted because
they are simply in close proximity due to their conditions of employment, rather
than in the reciprocal way suggested by the notion of 'intermediary' activity.

There are also indications of significant knowledge gaps, and clear evidence
that employees engaged in intermediary activity – knowledge workers, those
working with information and symbols – are involved in attempting to plug these
gaps. If the work of cultural intermediaries entails the production and circulation
of information and symbolic materials, so it also involves the concealment of
knowledge, deception and manipulation (widespread within advertising and
marketing, and at its most apparent in some of the publicity and public relations
work to be found in the music and film industries). As Arjun Appadurai has
observed, as artifacts move over ever greater distances from producers to consumers 'so the negotiation of the tension between knowledge and ignorance
becomes itself a critical determinant of the flow of commodities' (1986: 41). As
this occurs, cultural intermediaries are required to find ways of becoming ever
more adept at masking and obscuring this tension between corporate knowledge
and public ignorance. It is, therefore, important that research does not neglect
the full range of conditions and practices entailed in this type of intermediary
activity, particularly those deliberate attempts to distort and conceal information, or circulate false ideas.

I have been making a number of general points in this section, two I wish to
stress. First, the emphasis on a certain conception of cultural intermediaries
tends to result in other occupations not appearing in the frame, occupations that
are crucial to the commercial and institutional mediation of cultural forms, practices and artifacts (and certainly for an understanding of the mediations of pro-
duction/consumption within contemporary capitalism). Whilst it would be
unhelpful to broaden the category of 'cultural intermediaries' to include such
other workers and activities, we should certainly not draw an artificial boundary
around these privileged symbolic practices and neglect the way they are inte-
grated into and operate in direct relation to a range of intermediary activities.
Second, the focus on this specific conception of cultural intermediaries fails to
adequately interrogate the gaps or spaces between production and consumption.
It takes the apparent symbolic fit between producer and consumer (the presumed
effectiveness of publicity and 'consumer intelligence') at face value, and neglects
how the growth of a cluster of 'culture industries' dependent upon advertising
imagery, promotional techniques and marketing methods have 'widened the
distance . . . between producers and consumers' (Garnham, 2000: 162). The
increasing use of publicity, public relations and marketing, and other symbolic
intermediary activity, has not necessarily resulted in production and consumption being brought closer together. Instead, it has exaggerated the space between
the product (or performer) and the public. Cultural intermediaries are

frequently offered to us as workers who are filling this gap and making the connection. But, like much of the imagery, words and symbols they are engaged in constructing and circulating, they offer the illusion of such a link rather than its material manifestation. Cultural intermediaries reproduce rather than bridge the distance between production and consumption.

How creative, active and reflexive are cultural intermediaries?

The workers who are characterized as cultural intermediaries tend to be accorded an active, self-conscious, reflexive and creative role in their particular activities. This accent is apparent in the writings of Bourdieu and Mike Featherstone, and also in the work of those authors who have adopted this concept in their research (e.g. O'Connor and Wynne, 1996). This emphasis seems even more so now that there is a distinct tendency to speak of the 'creative industries', a trend that the British Labour Government has both latched on to and has been instrumental in propagating as part of its economic and cultural policies. Yet many of the practices that have been identified here, and subject to academic study, might involve activities that are rather more habitual and routine than has sometimes been implied or described. On this point it might be work relocating the work of cultural intermediaries and placing it within a longer tradition of thinking about the occupational practices of people who intervene between production and consumption, particularly those involved in the arts, media and formal institutions of cultural production (if, as is assumed, 'cultural intermediaries' are most prominent in advertising, radio, television, print journalism and the general circulation of symbolic forms).

Up until the 1970s and into the 1980s, research into the working worlds of media organizations and commercial cultural production, was dominated by the concerns of occupational sociologists and mass communication researchers and, despite being subject to considerable critique, this type of research has by no means disappeared. There is a substantial body of work that focuses on those involved in 'boundary spanning roles', a term used by Paul Hirsch (1972) in writings published during the late 1960s and early 1970s when he focused on the music business, book publishing and film industries. Hirsch thought of the linkages between production and consumption through the metaphors of 'filters' and 'flows' and by utilizing the concept of the gatekeeper. As is well known (for an overview see Tumber, 1999; McQuail, 1994), this notion emerged in early communication studies of the 'production of news' and was initially posited as a challenge to the idea that news is simply a reflection of events 'out there' in the world. The gatekeeper concept sought to stress the editorial selection of very particular stories and hence the production of partial versions of complex events. Although developed from the study of news, a generalized model of the gatekeeper was adopted by various writers seeking to stress how key personnel control access to cultural production: the editors who decide which authors will have their books selected for publication; the talent scouts who decide which songs and recordings will be selected; or producers who decide which movie ideas or scripts will be developed (see Ettema and Whitney, 1982).

Taken alone, the gatekeeper concept is limited by the assumption that cultural items simply appear at the 'gates' of the media or culture producing corporation where they are either admitted or excluded. Not only is content actively sought out (someone has to go and find the talent or the story), it can be systematically planned, with staff in the organization deciding in advance the genre of story, music or film they are seeking and encouraging its internal construction or sub-contracted production. However, if linked with an awareness of the various internal occupational routines and organizational values guiding the construction of cultural artifacts within organizations, this literature can be useful for providing an insight into the habits and routines within media and culture producing organizations. Indeed, perhaps one of its key insights is to highlight how symbolic material is constructed as a result of very well established routines that require little effort or sourcing (up-dating old stories, re-writing old songs, re-packaging old programmes or novels). Such routines make working life easier (enabling workers to deal with the pressure of time, deadlines and production schedules – to keep the presses rolling or the manufacturing plant running). These routines also introduce a sense of certainty or predictability into the process, encouraging the adherence to formulas and patterns of working that have proved successful in the past. Whilst much of the literature that focuses on these processes is far removed from debates about the activities of new cultural intermediaries it is clearly relevant to any consideration of the occupational activities of this class fraction, and would suggest that a large amount of work involving 'symbolic goods and services' may be conducted through the adherence to standardized occupational formulas and generic conventions, and operating within rather than across the boundaries of organizations.

In signposting this body of research I am not suggesting that such routines simply dominate or that this should be a sole focus of attention. I am arguing that any study of cultural intermediaries should incorporate an awareness of the research that has stressed the habitual, unreflexive and uncritical adherence to well established production routines and occupational formulae (even if many of these ideas might seem lost amongst some of the less inspiring writings about 'mass communication'). In arguing this I am also not implying that more recent research has not challenged this body of work, nor shown its various limitation. My point is rather to argue that we should develop an ability to untangle or disaggregate the practices of cultural intermediaries: to work out when, how and under what conditions such aesthetic activity might be creative, innovative and providing any more than an impetus inclining towards the conservative and mundane. This seems particularly important if we take it, as Nixon (1996, 1997) suggests in his writings on this subject, that these workers have been judged to manifest certain progressive tendencies that challenge existing social and cultural hierarchies. There is perhaps a need for a greater sense of when and how the routines, habits and codes are broken or maintained; by who, in what ways and with what consequences.

Strategies of inclusion and exclusion

In his writing on the role of advertising practitioners, Nixon (1997) has also argued that we need a more 'differentiated picture' of cultural intermediaries, one which is sensitive to differences aligned with educational background and training, and which is aware of issues of gender and race. I endorse this point, but would go further and ask that we question some of the assumptions about the pluralism, and fluidity of movement into the occupations of those involved in new forms of cultural production, particularly some of the assumptions about their apparent openness.

In Bourdieu's formulation, cultural intermediaries are characterized as occupying a position where 'jobs and careers have not yet acquired the rigidity of the older bureaucratic professions' (Bourdieu, 1984: 151). Entry into these occupations is usually via networks of connections, shared values and common life experiences. Gaining access to work is less dependent upon a meritocracy or assessment and recruitment according to formal qualifications. Bourdieu's conclusions were reached following empirical research conducted in the 1960s, yet this point has been continually stressed by subsequent writers. For example, Justin O'Connor, taking up this theme, writes of how cultural intermediaries become ever more significant in contributing to social change in what he calls 'an a era of post-scarcity' when 'the cultural hierarchies are much more fragmented and plural' (1999: 7).

But, to what extent is this any more or less open? We need to ask more questions here about who is admitted or excluded, how this occurs and how it might vary across different arts and media industries. Anecdotally, there is much evidence (in biographies, trade magazines and so on) to suggest that the film industry, for example, is dominated by very strong family connections. Not only are actors and actresses often drawn from very well established family dynasties, so too are producers and directors. In a newspaper profile of the actress Sigourney Weaver, to cite one case, it becomes clear that the recognition of her talent and her subsequent success has been facilitated by the environment, economic support and cultural capital provided by a 'family background' of 'entertainment aristocracy' (Mackenzie, 2000: 11). Less within the elite worlds of stardom, in my own work on the music industry in Britain I have found clear connections between aesthetic hierarchies, working practices within companies and broader class divisions.

Researching in the late 1980s and then into the 1990s (Negus, 1992, 1999),

I found that most of the key decision makers within the British music industry shared many features in common and have come to constitute a coherent class grouping. Those executives who have been in the business for 25–30 years and who find themselves in senior management or running labels have been drawn from a very particular class background and habitus. Recruited into the music industry during the 1960s and early 1970s, most senior executives are middle-class, white males who have received a privately funded education at 'public schools', or attended state grammar schools, and completed studies at university. Their formative experience has been shaped during the era when rock was gaining cultural value, becoming self-consciously intellectual and respectable; an epoch when various elements of rhythm and blues and rock'n'roll were 'appropriated' and 'rechristened rock or progressive music by its recently enfranchised grammar school, student and hip middle class audience' (Chambers, 1985: 84). A simultaneous expansion of the universities and institutions of cultural production provided an impetus that facilitated the recruitment into the recording industry of a group of mildly bohemian young people associated with the 'counter-culture'. Many of these young executives had initially been involved in booking bands, often as university entertainment officers, and a considerable number had played in rock bands. The 'genre culture' of British rock music provided a particular series of orientations, assumptions, dispositions and values, and these were carried into the organizations of music production and came to dominate agendas within the expanding recording industry. Despite often being presented as a fairly 'liberal' business, populated by personnel who are 'in touch with the street', these agendas were in no way a 'reflection' of the diversity of music being played and listened to in Britain. Instead they represented, in condensed form, the preferences and judgements of a small, relatively elite educated, middle-class, white male faction.

The aesthetic and social consequences of this have been profound. At a decisive phase in its expansion and growth, the British music industry was re-organized around a series of dichotomies in which rock artists were favoured over pop or soul performers; albums were favoured over singles and self-contained bands or 'solo artists' who were judged, from a position derived from Romanticism, to 'express' themselves through writing their own songs were favoured over the more collaborative ways in which singers or groups of performers have, for many years, worked with arrangers, session musicians and songwriters in putting together a 'package'. Most obviously, conventional white male guitar bands were treated as long-term propositions, whilst soul and rhythm and blues music came to be treated in a more ad-hoc and casual manner. These distinctions not only informed acquisition policies and marketing philosophies, they were hierarchically inscribed into the drawing up of contracts, and the allocation of investment to departments, genres and artists.

In acquiring new artists, staff in the British music industry have not been responding, in any neutral or obvious way, to the 'talent available' or to 'public demand'. Equally, the working practices that have been institutionalized and which result in these aesthetic and commercial hierarchies are not explicable in terms of formal occupational titles nor straight forward arguments about the type of pressures exerted by the corporate capitalist control of production and distribution. These working practices have emerged and been shaped historically, as a result of broader social divisions within Britain and as a consequence of how the beliefs, practices and aesthetic dispositions of those cultural intermediaries who constitute a 'rock genre culture' have contributed to the formation of a particular type of music industry. These cultural intermediaries, whilst defying certain conventional divisions between work/leisure, continue to maintain boundaries of access and inclusion. Crucial here is the way that these workers have used their access to the cultural industries to maintain a series of rather more traditional and enduring boundaries, social divisions and hierarchies.

If these strategies of class exclusion have characterized the music industry (often considered to be one of the most accessible and liberal of businesses) then it is clear that comparable patterns can be found in other industries involved in providing symbolic goods and services. A case in point is presented by James Curran (2000) in his account of the frameworks of cultural values and social networks that bind together magazine and newspaper literary editors, publishers and novelists. Currans' study provides an example of how a relatively small literary network shapes the acquisition, hierarchical promotion and critical judgements made about books and authors. A range of biographical and anecdotal material suggests that this is also the case in the theatre and the fine arts.

With this in mind, my final point is to ask to what extent the activities and lifestyles of cultural intermediaries have posed any challenge to traditional elites or dominant classes? To what degree do the new cultural intermediaries make use of well established and rather more traditional ways of maintaining power, position, privilege and patronage? These are questions that surely need to be addressed via a thorough analysis of the power relations involved, if we are to gain a fuller understanding of the consequences of the working practices that are proliferating at the moment where production meets consumption. Particularly if, as is implied in much of the writing on cultural intermediaries, a cultural politics is presumed to be possible at the point where production/consumption articulate, at the connecting point rather than within the discrete arenas of consumption (resistance and appropriation) or production (ownership and control). With its emphasis on the broader social significance, creativity and potential autonomy of a specific section of workers engaged in 'providing symbolic goods and services', it is perhaps ironic that the notion of 'cultural intermediaries' has been adopted from the work of Bourdieu, yet deployed in a manner that is prone to a strand of romanticism quite at odds with Bourdieu's project.

References

Appadurai, Arjun (1986) 'Introduction: commodities and the politics of value'. In A. Appadurai (ed.) *The Social Life of Things*. Cambridge: Cambridge University Press, 3–63.

Bourdieu, Pierre (1984) *Distinction. A Social Critique of the Judgment of Taste*. London: Routledge.

—— (1993) *The Field of Cultural Production*. Cambridge: Polity.

—— (1996) *The Rules of Art*. Cambridge: Polity.

Chambers, Iain (1985) *Urban Rhythms, Pop Music and Popular Culture*. Basingstoke: Macmillan.

Curran, James (2000) 'Literary editors, social networks and cultural tradition'. In J. Curran (ed.) *Media Organisations in Society*: London: Arnold, 215–39.

Du Gay, Paul (1996) *Consumption and Identity at Work*. Sage: London.

Du Gay, Paul, Hall, Stuart, Janes, Linda, Mackay, Hugh and Negus, Keith (1997) *Doing Cultural Studies: The Story of the Sony Walkman*. London: Sage.

Ettema, James and Whitney, D. Charles (eds) (1982) *Individuals in Mass Media Organizations: Creativity and Constraint*. London: Sage.

Featherstone, Mike (1991) *Consumer Culture and Postmodernism*. London: Sage.

Garcia Canclini, Nestor (1982) *Las Culturas Populares en el Capitalismo*. Mexico: Nueva Imagen.

—— (1993) *Transforming Modernity: Popular Culture in Mexico*. Austin, TX: University of Texas Press.

Garnham, Nicholas (2000) *Emancipation, the Media and Modernity*. Oxford: Oxford University Press.

Hirsch, Paul (1972) 'Processing fads and fashions: an organisational set analysis of cultural industry systems'. *American Journal of Sociology*, 77(4): 639–59.

Hofstede, Geert (1991) *Cultures and Organizations*. London: McGraw-Hill International.

Jones, T. C. (1995) *Accounting and the Enterprise*. London: Routledge.

Mackenzie, Suzie (2000) 'In a galaxy of her own'. *The Guardian Weekend*, 22 April, 10–15.

McQuail, Denis (1994) *Mass Communication Theory*. London: Sage.

McRobbie, Angela (1998) *British Fashion Design*. London: Routledge.

Negus, Keith (1992) *Producing Pop: Culture and Conflict in the Popular Music Industry*. London: Arnold.

—— (1995) 'Where the mystical meets the market; commerce and creativity in the production of popular music'. *The Sociological Review*, 47(2): 316–41.

—— (1998) 'Cultural production and the corporation: musical genres and the strategic management of creativity in the US recording industry'. *Media, Culture and Society*, 20(3): 359–79.

—— (1999) *Music Genres and Corporate Cultures*. London: Routledge.

Nixon, Sean (1996) *Hard Looks: Masculinities, Spectatorship and Contemporary Consumption*. London: UCL Press.

—— (1997) 'Circulating culture'. In P. du Gay (ed.) *Production of Culture/Cultures of Production*. London: Sage, 177–234.

O'Connor, Justin (1999) 'Popular culture, reflexivity and urban change'. In Jan Ver-wijnen and Panu Lehtovouri (eds) *Creative Cities: Cultural Industries, Urban Development and The Information Society*. Helsinki: University of Art and Design.

O'Connor, Justin and Wynne, Derek (eds) (1996) *From the Margins to the Centre: Cultural Production and Consumption in the Post-Industrial City*. Aldershot: Arena, Ashgate.

Peterson, Richard (1976) 'The production of culture. A prolegomenon'. In R. Peterson (ed.) *The Production of Culture*. London: Sage, 7–22.

Ryan, John and Peterson, Richard (1982) 'The product image: the fate of creativity in country music songwriting'. In J. Ettema and D. Whitney (eds) *Individuals in Mass Media Organizations: Creativity and Constraint*. London: Sage, 11–32.

Sartre, Jean Paul (1976) *Critique of Dialectical Reason*. London: NLB.

Tumber, Howard (ed.) (1999) *News: A Reader*. Oxford: Oxford University Press.

CULTURAL STUDIES 16(4) 2002, 516–531

Routledge
Taylor & Francis Group

Angela McRobbie

CLUBS TO COMPANIES: NOTES ON THE DECLINE OF POLITICAL CULTURE IN SPEEDED UP CREATIVE WORLDS

Abstract

This article proposes a recent acceleration in the nature and pace of work and employment in the UK culture industries. Multi-skilling and de-specialization are a result of growth, change and competition in the arts and media sector. Creative work increasingly follows the neo-liberal model, governed by the values of entrepreneurialism, individualization and reliance on commercial sponsorship. One consequence for the relatively youthful workforce is the decline of workplace democracy and its replacement by 'network sociality', which in turn is influenced by the lingering impact of dance and club culture. Independent work finds itself squeezed, compromised or brokered by the venture capitalists of culture as government encourages the 'freedom' allowed by this kind of labour.

Keywords

culture industries; club culture; network sociality; individualization; incubator

The 'Arts Labs' of the new cultural economy

Creative Industry Sectors as defined in Creative Industries Mapping Document,

Cultural Studies ISSN 0950-2386 print/ISSN 1466-4348 online © 2002 Taylor & Francis Ltd
http://www.tandf.co.uk/journals
DOI: 10.1080/09502380210139098

(DCMS, 1998): music, performing arts, publishing software, TV and radio, film, designer fashion, advertising, arts and antiques, crafts, design, architecture, interactive leisure software.

Cultural Entrepreneur Club (initiative led by ICA, London, Nesta, Arts Council England, Goldsmiths College London and Cap Gemini Ernst and Young, 2000): selected 'new job' titles of 400 invited members including arts promoter, incubator, consultancy for inventor, cultural strategist, multimedia artist, visual support consultant, media initiatives and relationships, digital design consultant, branding and communications, arts in business consultants, art-to-go sales, events organizer, new media agent, net casting/e label/cdrom, music portal, dance/music/youth culture, bio-entrepreneur.[1]

THIS ARTICLE PROVIDES a preliminary and thus provisional account of some of the defining characteristics of work and employment in the new cultural sector of the UK economy, and in London in particular.[2] It also describes a transition from what can be labeled 'first wave' culture industry work as defined by the Department of Culture, Media and Sport's creative industries document published in 1998 (see above) to the more economically highly-charged and rapidly mutating 'second wave' of cultural activity that has come into being in the last three years. This latter development is marked by de-specialization, by intersection with Internet working, by the utilizing of creative capacities provided by new media, by the rapid growth of multi-skilling in the arts field, by the shrunken role of the sector that I would describe as the 'independents', by a new partnership between arts and business with public sector support, and by government approval as evident in the most recently published Green Paper from the DCMS (2001).[3] (For new job titles see above). The 'second wave' comes into being as a consequence of the more rapid capitalization of the cultural field as small scale previously independent micro-economies of culture and the arts find themselves the subject of intense commercial interest.

The expansion of these sections of employment also brings about, for a more substantial number of people, a decisive break with past expectations of work.[4] Given the extensive press and television coverage of these kinds of work, a wider section of the population has available to it new ideas about how working lives can or might now be conducted. Through the profusion of profiles and interviews with hairdressers, cooks, artists and fashion designers, the public (especially young people) are presented with endless accounts of the seemingly inherent rewards of creative labour.[5] The flamboyantly *auteur* relation to creative work that has long been the mark of being a writer, artist, film director or fashion designer is now being extended to much wider section of a highly 'individuated' workforce. The media has always glamorized creative individuals as uniquely talented 'stars'. It is certainly not the case that now, in post-industrial Britain, people genuinely have the chance to fulfil their creative dreams. Rather it is the case that there is a double process of individualization. First, this occurs in the obsessive celebrity culture of the commercial media, now thoroughly extended to artists, designers and other creative personnel, and second in the social structure itself, as people are increasingly disembedded from ties of kinship, community and social class. They are, in a de-regulated environment, 'set free', as Giddens would put it, from both workplace organizations and from social institutions (Giddens, 1991).

What individualization means sociologically is that people increasingly have to become their own micro-structures, they have to do the work of the structures by themselves, which in turn requires intensive practices of self-monitoring or 'reflexivity'. This process where structures (like the welfare state) seem to disappear and no longer play their expected roles, and where individuals are burdened by what were once social responsibilities, marks a quite profound social transformation as Bauman, Beck and others have argued (Bauman, 1999, 2000; Beck, 2000). In the British context, this process of individualization could summarily be defined as the convergence of the forcefulness of neo-liberal economics put in place by the Thatcher government from 1979 onwards, with mechanisms of social and demographic change that result in new social groupings replacing traditional families, communities and class formations. Individualization is not about individuals *per se*, as about new, more fluid, less permanent social relations seemingly marked by choice or options. However, this convergence has to be understood as one of contestation and antagonism. Individualization thus marks a space of social conflict, it is where debates about the direction of change are played out and where new contradictions arise. This is most apparent in the world of work since it is here that the convergence is most dramatically configured. Capital finds novel ways of offloading its responsibility for a workforce, but this relinquishing process is confronted no longer by traditional and organized 'labour'. Instead, the new conditions of work are largely being experienced by 'new labour'. By this I mean those sections of the working population for whom work has become an important source for self-actualization, even freedom and independence. This includes women for whom work is an escape from traditional marriage and domesticity, young people for whom it is increasingly important as a mark of cultural identity, and ethnic minorities for whom it marks the dream of upward mobility and a possible escape from denigration.

The cultural sphere provides an ideal space for young people to explore such individualized possibilities, just as it also offers the Government opportunities for a post-industrialized economy unfettered by the constraints and costs of traditional employment. The impact of this intersection accounts for what I want to propose here as an acceleration in the cultural realm. There is a much expanded workforce comprising of freelance, casualized and project-linked persons, and there is also a more fiercely neo-liberal model in place with the blessings of government for overseeing the further de-regulation and commercialization of the cultural and creative sector (DCMS, 2001). The culture industries are being 'speeded up' and further capitalized as the state steps back and encourages the privatization of previously publicly subsidized cultural provision. (For example, by buying in freelance arts administrators for single projects, rather than employing full time staff.) Those working in the creative sector cannot simply rely on old working patterns associated with art worlds, they have to find new ways of 'working' the new cultural economy, which increasingly means holding down three or even four 'projects' at once.[6] In addition, since these projects are usually short term, there have to be other jobs to cover the short-fall when a project ends. The individual becomes his or her own enterprise, sometimes presiding over two separate companies at the one time.[7] To sum up, if we consider the creative industries in the UK as a kind of experimental site, or case study, or indeed 'arts lab' for testing out the possibilities for 'cultural entrepreneurialism' (see Leadbeater and Oakley, 1999), then I would suggest that we can also see a shift from first to second wave that in turn (ironically) marks the decline of 'the indies' (the independents), the rise of the creative subcontractor and the downgrading of creativity.

On the guest list? Club culture sociality at work

Given the ongoing nature of these developments, the authorial voice of the following pages is tentative in that I am drawing on observations and trends emerging from my current work in progress on this topic. I propose a number of intersecting and constitutive features. First, imported into the creative sector are elements of youth culture, in particular those drawn from the energetic and entrepreneurial world of dance and rave culture. Second, the realm of 'speeded up' work in the cultural sector now requires the holding down of several jobs at the one time; third, that such working conditions are also reliant on intense self promotional strategies, and, as in any business world, on effective 'public relations', and fourth, that where there is a new relation of time and space there is little possibility of a politics of the workplace. That is, there is little time, few existing mechanisms for organization, and anyway no fixed workplace for a workplace politics to develop. This throws into question the role and function of 'network sociality' (Wittel, 2002). Thus fifth and finally, we can see a manifest tension for new creative workers, highly reliant on informal networking but without the support of these being underpinned by any institutional 'trade association'. They can only find individual (or 'biographical' as Beck puts it) solutions to systemic problems (Beck, 1997).

The dance/rave culture that came into being in the late 1980s as a mass phenomenon has strongly influenced the shaping and contouring, the energizing and entrepreneurial character of the new culture industries. The scale and spread of this youth culture meant that it was more widely available than its more clandestine, rebellious, 'underground' and style-driven predecessors, including punk. The level of self-generated economic activity that 'dance-party-rave' organizations entailed, served as a model for many of the activities that were a recurrent feature of 'creative Britain' in the 1990s. Find a cheap space, provide music, drinks, video, art installations, charge friends and others on the door, learn how to negotiate with police and local authorities and in the process become a club promoter and cultural entrepreneur. This kind of activity was to become a source of revenue for musicians and DJs first, but soon afterwards for artists. It has meant that the job of 'events organizer' is one of the more familiar of new self-designated job titles. The form of club sociality that grew out of the ecstasy-influenced 'friendliness' of the clubbing years gradually evolved into a more hard-nosed networking, so that an informal labour market has come into being which takes as its model the wide web of contacts, 'zines', flyers, 'mates', grapevine and 'word of mouth' socializing that was also a distinctive feature of the 'micro-media' effects of club culture (Thornton, 1996). The intoxicating pleasures of leisure culture have now, for a sector of the under 35s, provided the template for managing an identity in the world of work. Apart from the whole symbolic panoply of jargon, clothes, music and identity, the most noted feature of this phenomenon was the extraordinary organizational capacity in the setting up and publicizing of 'parties'. Now that the existence of raves and dance parties has become part of the wider cultural landscape – having secured the interest and investment of major commercial organizations – it is easy to overlook the energy and dynamism involved in making these events happen in the first place. But the formula of organizing music, dance, crowd and space have subsequently proved to give rise to 'transferable skills', which in turn transform the cultural sector as it is also being opened up to a wider, younger and more popular audience.[8]

The example of the shaping-up influence of club culture, therefore, sets the scene for this article. And where patterns of self employment or informal work are the norm, what emerges is a radically different kind of labour market organiz-ation. While the working practices of graphic designers, website designers, events organizers, 'media office' managers and so on inevitably share some features in common with previous models of self-employed or freelance working, we can propose that where in the past the business side of things was an often disregarded aspect of creative identities best looked after by the accoun-tant, now it is perceived as integral and actively incorporated into the artistic identity. This is illustrated in the activities of the young British artists for whom the commercial aspect of the art world is no longer disparaged but is welcomed and even celebrated. Mentor and tutor to the Goldsmiths graduates (including Damien Hirst), Professor Michael Craig Martin reputedly encouraged the students to consider the partying and networking they had to do to promote their art as a vital part of the work, not as something separate.[9] He also insisted that artistic values were not incommensurate with entrepreneurial values. To some extent this more openly commercial approach is also part of the logic of breaking down the divide between high and low culture. If, for example, art is not such a special and exceptional activity, if it ought not to see itself as superior to the world of advertising, then what is to stop the artists from expecting the same kind of financial rewards, expense accounts and fees as the art directors inside the big agencies? The new relation between art and economics marks a break with past anti-commercial notions of being creative. Instead young people have exploited opportunities around them, in particular their facilities with new media technology and the experience of 'club culture sociality' with its attendant skills of networking and selling the self and have created for themselves new ways of earning a living in the cultural field.

In this creative economy, older features of working life such as the career pathway, the ladder of promotion, the 'narrative sociality' of a life spent in a strat-ified but secure workplace have been rapidly swept away to be replaced by 'network sociality' (Wittel, 2002). Work has been re-invented to satisfy the needs and demands of a generation who, 'disembedded' from traditional attach-ments to family, kinship, community or region, now find that work must become a fulfilling mark of self. In this context, more and more young people opt for the insecurity of careers in media, culture or art in the hope of success. In fields like film-making or fashion design there is a euphoric sense among practitioners of by-passing tradition, pre-empting conscription into the dullness of 9–5 and evading the constraints of institutional processes. There is a utopian thread embedded in this wholehearted attempt to make-over the world of work into something closer to a life of enthusiasm and enjoyment. We could also note that for young women, now entering into the labour market as a lifelong commit-ment instead of a part-time or interrupted accompaniment to family life as a primary career, the expectation that work is satisfying and inherently rewarding has a special significance alongside the need now to be one's own breadwinner.[10]

To have seemingly circumvented 'unhappy work' and to have come upon a way of earning a living without the feeling of being robbed of identity is a social phenomenon worthy of sociological attention. But the larger question of course is how this fits with the needs of a form of cultural capitalism that is currently re-inventing itself as innocuous or 'soft', at least in its Western forms. For the young woman fashion designer working 18 hour days and doing her own sewing to complete an order, 'loving' her work but self-exploiting herself, she only has herself to blame if things go wrong. After all she opted for this kind of unstable career choice.[11] This is exactly the scenario described by Bauman in his descrip-tion of the stealthy ways in which the new capitalism seems to absolve itself from responsibility by creating invisible structures, and by melting down or liquefying the old social order (Baumann, 1999). Self blame, where social structures are increasingly illegible or opaque, serves the interests of the new capitalism well, ensuring the absence of social critique.

A further defining feature of new cultural work is that its 'time and space' dynamics contribute to a marked absence of workplace politics in terms of democratic procedures, equal opportunities, anti-discrimination policies and so on. Maybe there can be no workplace politics when there is no workplace, i.e. where work is multi-sited. The necessity of speed and the velocity of transaction, along with the mobility and fluidity of individuals, throws into question a defining feature of this kind of work. This is its relation to the idea of 'reflexivity'. Underpinning both Giddens' and Beck's deployment of the concept is a traditional notion of the unified subject increasingly able – indeed called upon – to undertake self monitoring activities. But in both writers' use of the term, reflexivity has retained an abstract character, requiring us to ask, what are the limits of reflexive practice? Is reflexivity applied primarily to the job in hand? Or to put it another way, the socially valuable outcome of reflexivity is yet to reveal itself. We would need some ethnographies of reflexivity before it would be possible to draw any conclusions, or indeed before the actual mechanisms of reflexivity could be assessed. What are its parameters? Under what circumstances does it lead to social critique? If we alternately consider reflexivity as a form of self disciplining where subjects of the new enterprise culture are increasingly called upon to inspect themselves and their practices, in the absence of structures of social support (other than individualized counseling services), then reflexivity marks the space of self responsibility, self blame. In this sense, it is a de-politicizing, de-socializing mechanism: 'Where have I gone wrong?'

One way of explaining how and why things go wrong might involve turning to sociology. And, indeed, having recourse to specialist knowledge is how Beck understands reflexivity as operating. For him it is related to the wider dissemination and application of sophisticated sociological knowledge to the issues that sociology (or another academic field) has engaged with, usually as social problems and attempted to explain. (In the UK this is most apparent in the concept of the 'moral panic' in relation to youth culture; see McRobbie and Thornton, 1995.) Thus with an increasingly higher-educated population it might be surmised that critical reflexivity becomes a more widespread practice. But how does this tally with Bauman's argument that the more opaque the social structures of inequality and injustice, the less likely people are to understand how the society actually operates. At present, there is no obvious point of entrance for sociological explanations into these creative sectors since the trade media that covers these industries considers such knowledge as old fashioned or irrelevant. This is partly the result of the pervasive success of neo-liberal values, their insinuating presence in the culture and media sector, and their successful discrediting of the political vocabulary associated with the left and with feminism (including equal opportunities, anti-discrimination, workplace democracy, trade union representation, etc.). The only site for the dissemination of these values is the academy, the place of training or education of the creatives. But whether or not these are remembered or acted upon or cast aside is an open question. Only anecdotal evidence exists.[12]

The extent to which the new world of work contributes directly to the decline of political antagonism is a clear gain for the free market economy. In the cultural sector, with its emphasis on the creative and expressive, it might be imagined that this could be the right place for social minorities to succeed and for women to achieve equal participation. However it seems possible that quite the opposite is happening. What we see – in as much as it is possible to track these developments – is the emergence of working practices which reproduce older patterns of marginalization (of women and people from different ethnic backgrounds), while also disallowing any space or time for such issues to reach articulation.[13] In this case the club culture question of 'are you on the guest list?' is extended to recruitment and personnel, so that getting an interview for contract creative work depends on informal knowledge and contacts, often friendships. Once in the know about who to approach (the equivalent of finding where the party is being held), it is then a matter of whether the recruitment advisor 'likes you' (the equivalent of the bouncer 'letting you in'), and all ideas of fairness or equal representation of women or of black or Asian people (not to mention the disabled) fly out of the window.

In this new and so-called independent sector (see Leadbeater and Oakley, 1999) there is less and less time left in the long hours culture to pursue 'independent work'. The recent attempts by the large corporations to innovate in this sector means that the independents are, in effect, dependent sub-contracted suppliers. And where such contracts are to be had, in a context of increasing competition, it is hard to imagine that there is time and space for private reading never mind wider critical debate. (As Lash and Urry comment, 'information technology can . . . erode the critical crafts of reading and writing. What Agger calls 'fast capitalism' undermines the power of the book', (1994: 324).) And after-hours, in the dedicated club/networking space, with free vodka on tap all night thanks to the sponsorship of the big drinks companies, who dares to ask 'uncool' questions about the minimal representation of women and non-white young people, about who the big clients are and what they do with the product, and about the downside of the 'talent-led' economy? In an atmosphere of businesslike conviviality overseen by accomplished 'PRs', the emphasis on presentation of self is incompatible with a contestatory demeanour. It's not cool to be 'difficult'. Personal angst, nihilism or mere misgivings must be privately managed and, for the purposes of club sociality, carefully concealed.[14] This is a 'PR' meritocracy where the question of who gets ahead on what basis and who is left behind finds no space for expression. Speed and risk negate ethics, community and politics.

The demise of the indies?

Given the picture that I have been sketching, it is incumbent upon social scientists and cultural studies academics to develop a vocabulary and a methodology for tracing freelance pathways in the cultural sector. We need to be able to understand at the level of experience how this terrain is negotiated. There remains a chasm of difference between middle-aged academics for whom the university sector has provided a single sourced income more or less since graduation, and young people whose portfolio careers increasingly mean not serial jobs but multi-tasking. The latter becomes necessary partly because there is no cushion of welfare to cover periods between jobs, also because labour costs are falling in the cultural sector, and finally because creative work, as various studies have shown, is simply low pay work except for those at the very top.[15] Since 1998 I have been engaged in a tracking research study of freelance, self employed and contract creative workers (a handful of whom are fashion designers who participated in my earlier study (see McRobbie, 1998)). For them the kind of conditions which prevailed in the 'independent' cultural scene in London and in other UK cities between 1986–1996 are very much a thing of the past. Despite the hardship faced by the fashion designers I interviewed, including the long hours and the difficulties of maintaining a cash flow, the luxury they had, as my more recent respondents see it, was of being able to concentrate on their 'own work'. This sector of independent fashion design has been swept away as the high street chains are able to translate the catwalk styles into off the peg items literally within days. Likewise with the spiraling of urban property values there are fewer opportunities for finding cheap centrally located market stalls. By the end of the 1990s the only way to be 'independent' was to be 'dependent' on Kookai, Debenhams, Top Shop. Indeed the only way fashion design could survive was to sign up with a bigger company and more or less relinquish 'creative independence'. The corrosion of creativity was further achieved as the chain stores 'adopted' less than a handful of graduate stars a year and often discarded them within the year. State support for young and struggling designers working from tiny outlets is no longer available following changes to the benefits system. Voluntary sector support is also limited. The Prince of Wales Trust, for example, only offers a loan scheme for up to £5,000 for the under 30s. As a consequence fashion designers become a scattered and disconnected profession. They can no longer be found in key city centre locations. The small shops are all gone. An important outlet like Hyper Hyper, a unit space for up and coming designers situated in Kensington High Street, London disappeared in 1998. What now happens to the annual crop of 4,000 fashion graduates who relied on this kind of space? The answer is that they are now advised to play safe and get a job with a high street retailer. A tiny number are recruited by the European fashion houses or by the American conglomerates, and one or two are awarded grants. Hence I think we can surmise that there is a decline in creativity, as the incubation period that was documented in my earlier research becomes increasingly unviable. There is nothing like the vibrancy and the collective (and competitive) spirit which characterized the earlier period. Fashion design graduates today must become multi-skilled. If they are doing a collection it will be at weekends, or perhaps in the odd day they can find between other jobs. Typically magazines like *I-D* find ways of celebrating this new scenario. In a recent article published in the magazine, the journalist wrote, 'Fashion multi-taskers: suddenly they're everywhere. . . . And its addictive. Once you've tried doing four jobs you'll never want anything less. . . . It's no longer necessary to be a full time anything to be successful and respected' (Rushton, 2001).

The substance and tone of this article reflects the kind of upbeat business-minded euphoria which is a characteristic of the sector. So much for reflexivity. When it is inconceivable that the main trade magazine shows itself capable of seriously reflecting on conditions in the sector, then magazines like *The Face, I-D* and *Dazed and Confused* demonstrate themselves to be remarkably disengaged and complicit with the changes affecting the industry. These changes come from the increased presence of the big brands. The large companies need to innovate and to develop a more experimental youth-driven image and this is provided by the second wave of young cultural entrepreneurs hiring out their services on a contractual basis. But what is squeezed out in this process is independence and socially engaged, critical creativity. The same is true for many other of the creative sectors. Freelance economies in the field of film or video production cannot, for example, take the strain of turning down work to free up time to make, let us say, a short documentary film uncommissioned and with no apparent destination. Instead cultural production is increasingly driven by the imperatives of market and consumer culture, and the banality of pop promos, TV and cinema advertising is concealed by the technological euphoria, the association of newness and youthfulness, and of course by the parties, the celebrity culture and the cheque in the post. Granted there are still fashion designers, architects, writers, musicians and other creative occupations, but being a specialist rather than a multi-skilled 'creative' is becoming a thing of the past and a mark of being over 35.[16] The norm now is a kind of middle class 'ducking and diving'. In the shift from the first to the second wave of creative economy in the New Labour enterprise culture, the kind of small scale economies of the decade from the mid 1980s to mid 1990s have all but disappeared. Thus we could say that the cultural entrepreneurialization set in motion during the Thatcher years has in the Blair period been almost fully accomplished. Of course it is important to avoid a crude determinism. It is not, therefore, my intention to engage here with questions of cultural value, but rather to point to a process of creative compromise. There is more and more culture, more visual work, more novels being published, more music being produced, more magazines being launched and at the same time the shift from there being 'independent work' to there being any number of freelance workers is also a shift in the balance of power from a social 'milieu of innovation' to a world of individual 'projects'.

The loneliness of the long distance incubator

Let me conclude by rehearsing some of the features that serve to consolidate the new (and rarely spoken about) structural divides in the cultural economy. If the club is the hub, then age and domestic responsibilities define patterns of access and participation. While sociologists have pointed to the increasing impact of age in changing labour markets (especially for women; see Walby, 1997) in the creative sector, there is simultaneously a stretching out of the contours of youthfulness (such as 'middle youth') through the marketing of lifestyle goods to the under 50s, and also a retrenchment and re-marking of boundaries, in that the new ways of working bear the hallmark of the rave culture generation. The nighttime economy of club culture translates directly into the long hours culture of new media and creative work. This is obviously incompatible with having children, and certainly incompatible with being, for example, a single parent. Work merges with leisure and when a deadline must be met friends might lend their support and work through the night (McRobbie, 1998). The assumed youthfulness and the impregnable space of the club suggests that these are not such 'open-minded' spaces. Of course, all occupational groups develop their own ways of working, and nor is the club a novelty for artistic and creative persons *per se*. But there is an irony in that alongside the assumed openness of the network, the apparent embrace of non-hierarchical working practices, the various flows and fluidities (see Lash and Urry, 1994), there are quite rigid closures and exclusions. The cultural and creative sectors have in the past in the UK been led and administered by the public sector. Academics have also had a role to play. But a close reading of the recent Green Paper 'Culture and Creativity Ten Years On' (DCMS, 2001) implies that this will change dramatically, as artists and creative individuals are freed from the constraints of bureaucracy and 'red tape'. As the whole sector is more thoroughly entrepreneurialized there will be less need for the infrastructure of state, indeed it is argued that it will be to the advantage of the artists that administration will be cut. The result? Artists and cultural personnel will be free to carry on with what they do unhindered. Academics will be kept well out of the picture, indeed if the recent Cultural Entrepreneur Club is a model, their presence will be occasional and by invitation only. What warrants the presence of those who are not 'good for business'?[17]

The second structural dynamic is that of qualification. The conventions associated with the traditional CV and the job application process are nothing short of overturned in the network culture, and yet patterns do re-emerge. Top or 'branded' universities promise graduates better access to big companies seeking to outsource creative work, and the same holds true for appointments with venture capitalists. Universities and colleges become key sites for developing the social skills for the network (once again often as party organizer), so, for the 45% of young people who at present do not enjoy three years of higher education, this is a further absence of opportunity. (It is also unlikely that mature students who are concentrated in poorer universities are in the position to immerse themselves in the hedonistic and expensive culture of networking.) Third, there is the spatial dynamic, with only a few urban centres providing anything like the cultural infrastructure for gainful employment in creative fields. With a handful of private–public partnerships now replacing the kind of city cultural policies for regeneration pursued in the 1980s and into the early 1990s, there is the appearance of shadow culture industries in Glasgow, Manchester and Nottingham (all of which are have large student populations) while, as Lead-beater reports (1999), Cardiff Bay has also seen the development of a thriving new media sector. But this leaves vast tracks of the country more or less untouched by the work opportunities provided by the cultural and creative network and it creates an enormous imbalance between London where, at least on the short term, freelance curators and art project managers can have five jobs on the go at once (and thus juggle the bank balance around the cash-flow) and elsewhere where 'portfolio income' is replaced by at best 'one job at a time', usually with spaces of no work in between. (Is London also disembedded and individuated, a city state with its own speeded up economy? What distortions occur as a result of this 'lifted out' status?)

Age, gender, ethnicity, region and family income re-emerge like phantoms (or in Beck's terminology 'zombie concepts', dead but still alive) from the dis-guised hinterland of this new soft capitalism and add their own weight to the life chances of those who are attempting to make a living in these fields (Beck, 2000). As Adkins (1999) argues, new forms of re-traditionalisation begin to have an impact on the participation of disadvantaged social groups and minorities. Adkins is suggesting that where state provided supports disappear and community weakens, and where individuated persons operate on a more self reliant basis, in this case in the new cultural economy, then there will almost inevitably be a process of having to fall back on traditional forms of support. This can mean a return to more rigid gender roles for women, for example, being excluded from the network because of children, or finding it difficult to avoid reproducing tra-ditionally patriarchal family forms. Such changes are also the result of the double process of neo-liberal successes in the field of work and the negating of the values of the left and the women's movement. Finally there is the sheer incommensu-rability of working patterns in the creative network with existing official, govern-mental and social science paradigms. (Even the recent Green Paper fails to appreciate the growth of multi-taskers in the arts.) There is as yet no category for the curator/project manager/artist/website designer who is transparently multi-skilled and ever willing to pick up new forms of expertise, who is also con-stantly finding new niches for work and thus inventing new jobs for him/herself (e.g. incubator/creative agent), who is highly mobile moving from one job or project to the next, and in the process also moving from one geographical site to the next. Social interaction is fast and fleeting, friendships need to be put on hold, or suspended on trust and when such a non-category of multi-skilled persons is extended across a whole sector of young working people, there is a sharp sense of transience, impermanence and even solitude (Auge, 1995).

Research on these areas would have to consider the specifically gendered and ethnic consequences of individualization. The existing methodologies of the social sciences might well be brought into crisis by the fluidity and hyper-mobility of these agents. There are a number of other points of tension or ambivalence that also throw our older political paradigms into crisis. In the past I have taken issue with those who have (often with a sneer) considered the ambition and energy, the glamour and desire for success on the part of these young people as evidence of their either being complicit with the aims and ambitions of the project set in motion by Mrs Thatcher, or else of their being ideologically bludgeoned into believing the Hollywood dream (McRobbie, 1999). My argument was that it was quite possible to adhere to principles of social justice, and gender and racial equality while working in the seemingly glamorous world of the culture industries. Of course, in the absence (yet again) of studies that systematically tracked creative employment with political sensibility, my comments were based on working closely with students who would be entering or who already had entered these fields. The accelerated speed of cultural working in the second wave, however, marks an intensification of individualization, a more determined looking out for the self. At this point the possibility of a revived, perhaps reinvented, radical democratic politics that might usefully de-individuate and resocialize the world of creative work is difficult to envisage.

To conclude, if the instruments of the social sciences are challenged by the flows of creative individuals, and likewise the vocabularies of social democratic practice seem ill-equipped for the new mobile work-sites of cultural capitalism, so also is it the case that the identity of these cultural workers as bounded by the characteristics of 'British creativity' is a quite profound misnomer. The creative work that central government in the UK wants to flag up is less British than is assumed.[18] Many are producing for a global market, as mobile subjects the political peculiarities of the nation state begin to look either insular, or restrictive, for example in relation to work practices and migration law. This undermines the value of a vocabulary of political culture bound by nation. The second wavers are redescribing culture and creativity as we know them, transcending and traversing a multiplicity of boundaries that come tumbling down in an 'ecstasy of communication'. We cultural studies academics might teach these young people in the relatively fixed space of the seminar room, but once they enter the world of work, our encounters with 'incubators' and others are increasingly estranged and contingent.

Acknowledgement

I am grateful to a wide network of former students who have commented on and refined the ideas here, especially Raj Thind and Jesh Hanspal.

Notes

1   This is taken from the guest list for the September 2000 meeting of the Cultural Entrepreneurs Club, attended by 325 people and hosted at Channel Four.

2   For London as a global city see Sassen (1995); for cultural economies and urban areas see Scott (2000).

3   By 'independents' I mean small scale micro-economies primarily in music and fashion and related fields, which emerged as post punk phenomena in the mid-1980s in response to unemployment and to government endorsement of 'enterprise culture'. Generally, these groupings presented themselves as radical, critical, innovative and loosely collective, e.g. the fashion duo Body Map, the 'indie' record label Rough Trade and the magazine *The Face* in its early days.

4   The DCMS Mapping Document (1998) indicates employment rates in culture and communication at over 1 million persons, the DCMS Mapping Document of 2001 puts the figure at 1.3 million.

5   In an earlier article on this subject I quoted a hairdresser interviewed in the *Independent* who said he was 'classically trained' (McRobbie, 1999).

6   This kind of comment is emerging from current interviews with respondents working in the cultural sector. They repeatedly tell me of small companies undercutting others by offering virtually no cost for jobs that will help their profile.

7   Another respondent currently runs one tiny TV production company, another media consultancy and alongside this she also teaches two days a week.

8   Rave culture is a much cited influence on the entrepreneurial activities of artists including Damien Hirst.

9   Personal communication from former MA student, Goldsmiths College London.

10   Young women are increasingly encouraged to consider work and employment as lifelong activities as partners can no longer be relied upon as breadwinners.

11   The Minister for Culture Media and Sports the Rt Hon Chris Smith actually suggested in a panel debate (Royal Television Society, February 1999) that the young people working in the industry 'do it because they love it, they know what they are letting themselves in for'.

12   An unexpected consequence of my study of UK fashion designers is that I have been visited by a stream of aspiring young fashion graduates who have come across the book and, as a result, seek my advice.

13   Cultural Entrepreneur Club (September/October/November 2000) comprised of a majority of white males from 'good' universities.

14   This point is made clearly in 'Good character and dressing for success' by Jesh Hanspal, unpublished MA Thesis Goldsmiths College (2000).

15   This is the result in my study McRobbie (1998), and also Ursell (2000).

16   At the above mentioned Cultural Entrepreneurs Club I was introduced to a trained architect working as a time-based arts agent, a photographer working as a curator/administrator and a graphic designer working as a website editor.

17   Again, on both occasions I attended this club I was the only academic present. Unlike the business mentors and venture capitalists also present, I found no immediate role to play other than to talk with former students.

18   The nominations for the Turner Prize 2000 included three non-UK artists, one German, one Dutch and another Japanese all based in London, and two of whom trained in London art colleges. In fact, a pattern is emerging where European and overseas student train in UK art colleges and then go on to enjoy better support for their creative activities from their own governments than is available in the UK. Hence the prominence of the new Dutch, Belgian and South Asian fashion designers.

References

Adkins, L. (1999) 'Community and economy: a retraditionalisation of gender'. *Theory Culture and Society*, 16(1): 119–41.

Auge, M. (1995) *Non-Places: Introduction to an Anthropology of Supermodernity*. London: Verso.

Bauman, Z. (1999) *Liquid Modernity*. Cambridge: Polity Press.

—— (2000) *The Individualised Society*. Cambridge: Polity Press.

Beck, U. (1997) *Risk Society*. London: Sage.

—— (2000) Unpublished lecture. LSE, February, London.

DCMS (1998) Creative Industries: Mapping Document, London.

—— (2001) Creative Industries Mapping Document, London.

Giddens, A. (1991) *Modernity and Self Identity*. Cambridge: Polity Press.

Hanspal, J. (2000) 'Good character and dressing for success'. Unpublished MA Thesis, Goldsmiths College, London.

Lash, S. and Urry, J. (1994) *The Economy of Signs and Spaces*. London: Sage.

Leadbeater, C. (1999) *Living on Thin Air*. London: Viking.

Leadbeater, C. and Oakley, J. (1999) *The Independents*. London: Demos.

McRobbie, A. (1998) *British Fashion Design: Rag Trade or Image Industry?* London: Routledge.

—— (1999) *In the Culture Society*. London: Routledge.

McRobbie, A. and Thorton, S. (1995) 'Rethinking "moral panic" for multi-mediated social worlds'. *British Journal of Sociology*, 66(4): 559–575.

Rushton, R. (2001) 'Fashion feature'. *I-D Magazine*, February.

Sassen, S. (1995) *The Global City*. Oxford: Blackwell.

Scott, A. (2000) *The Cultural Economy of Cities*. London: Sage.

Thornton, S. (1996) *Club Culture*. Cambridge: Polity Press.

Ursell, G. (2000) 'Television production: issues of exploitation, commodification and subjectivity in UK television labour markets'. *Media, Culture and Society*, 22(6): 805–827.

Walby, S. (1997) *Gender Transformations*. London: Routledge.

Wittel, A. (2001) 'Toward a network sociality'. *Theory Culture and Society*, 18(6): 51–77.

CULTURAL STUDIES 16(4) 2002, 532–552

Routledge
Taylor & Francis Group

Liz McFall

WHAT ABOUT THE OLD CULTURAL INTERMEDIARIES? AN HISTORICAL REVIEW OF ADVERTISING PRODUCERS

Abstract

Critical work on advertising is underscored by a teleological conception of its object. This often emerges in the form of an emphasis on advertising as an evolving, hybrid institutions that increasingly mixes the 'economic' with the 'cultural'. It is in this vein that advertising practitioners have been characterized as 'new cultural intermediaries' deploying distinctive aesthetic sensibilities. Similar patterns of knowledge and behaviour, however, can be traced amongst early producers of advertising suggesting a generation of 'old' cultural intermediaries. This unexpected phenomenon, it is argued, arises for two reasons. The first is that much critical work addressing the nature of contemporary advertising lacks historical context. The second is that culture and economy are normatively conceptualized as separate spheres. This separation underplays the multiple interconnections between the cultural and the economic in instances of material practice. Accordingly it is proposed that advertising be reformulated as a *constituent practice* that has historically relied upon the juxtaposition of 'cultural' and 'economic' knowledges.

Keywords

advertising history; cultural intermediaries; culture; economy; practice

Cultural Studies ISSN 0950-2386 print/ISSN 1466-4348 online © 2002 Taylor & Francis Ltd
http://www.tandf.co.uk/journals
DOI: 10.1080/09502380210139106

Introduction

SEAN NIXON'S DESCRIPTION of the 'magisterial centrality' of texts (1996: 200) in critical work on advertising captured an increasingly embarrassing tendency within the academy for detailed analyses of advertising to be carried out without any reference to the production context. Academic work has had an enduring preoccupation with the advertising text as the key source of meaning and therefore the appropriate object of analysis. This state of affairs has been effectively challenged by authors like Moeran (1996), Mort (1996), Miller (1997), Nixon (1996, 1997) and Slater (2000), who have sought in various ways to restore the production context to studies of advertising. This literature makes a substantial contribution to the theoretical profile of advertising and it has played a major role in awakening interest in the study of practices rather than texts. Nevertheless the aim in this article is to explore some of the questions provoked by this shift in critical emphasis. One of the unanticipated results of the breakaway from reliance on textual approaches, it is proposed, has been an inflation of the particular significance of contemporary forms of advertising practice. What the new attention to practice shares with textual approaches is the deeply rooted critical desire to understand the role played by advertising in contemporary societies. This has meant that many discussions of advertising practice have also engaged with broader diagnostic debates about the nature of the contemporary moment and the relation between the 'cultural' and the 'economic' within it.

In an attempt to give a sense of the weight of this theoretical tradition, the first section of this article considers how the culture/economy relation has been conceptualized in critical theory and how this has impacted on work focused on advertising generally and on advertising practice more specifically. The notion of the 'new cultural intermediary' is of particular interest here as it gave a lead to the characterization of advertising practitioners as occupying a new and uniquely hybrid 'cultural' and 'economic' position.

The second section aims to demonstrate that despite its apparent newness the cultural intermediary position is not unprecedented. With this in mind some of the ways in which early advertising producers acted as intermediaries are explored. In particular attention is drawn to how the working practices of advertising producers have been informed by their connections to particular aesthetic universes. The underlying argument is that the producers of advertising have historically, and in a variety of different ways, sought to use what might be termed 'cultural' knowledges to enhance the effectiveness of advertising.

The existence of 'old cultural intermediaries', it is proposed in the closing section, raises two main problems with the 'new cultural intermediary' as a theoretical category. The first and most straightforward of these concerns historical evidence. Recent attention to advertising practice is stamped by the broader critical desire to capture its 'epochal' significance. Yet most assertions about its profound difference from whatever has gone before are based not on historical description but on theoretical tradition. This side-stepping of history may be one reason why theorists see a little too much novelty in the culture/economy relation in their own wages. But a further more entrenched reason exists. This stems from the ingrained pattern of thought in which culture and economy appear as essentially separate domains. Historical and anthropological evidence, however, suggests multiple and inextricable links between the 'cultural' and the 'economic' in material practice. Viewed in this light, the mixed cultural and economic competencies of early advertising practitioners come as no surprise.

Contemporary advertising practitioners as an instance of the increasing hybridity of culture and economy

'Culture' and 'economy' are amongst the most problematic categories in the social and human sciences. They appear self-evident yet are enormously difficult to define. Each term is used to refer to both the most abstract dimensions of human experience and the most specific of daily transactions. The theoretical challenge of defining these categories precisely yet inclusively is not one to which this article can fully respond but one aspect of the way these terms are used in critique is taken up. That is the emphasis on culture and economy as *properly* separate and opposed 'spheres' or 'domains' of existence. An underlying aim here is to investigate this characterization and to work towards an alternative position that foregrounds the degree to which the 'cultural' and the 'economic' are entangled dimensions of practice rather than discrete spheres.

The idea that industrialization and the associated emergence of a consumer society acted to transform the relation between culture and economy has a long history. The 'Frankfurt School' saw the expansion of capitalist production as necessitating the construction of new markets based upon a commodification of culture primarily through media like advertising. Commodity logic and the instrumentalized rationality of industrialized systems for the mass production of goods, for Horkheimer and Adorno (1971), was also increasingly characteristic of the production of culture in the 'culture industries'. Culture here is debased by the commodity logic of capitalist systems of production. This logic involves the 'fetishization' of commodities and the triumph of 'exchange-value' over 'use-value'. The result, for many theorists, is an 'emptying out' of the real meanings of commodities in favour of those manufactured by advertising (Williamson, 1977; Haug 1986; Jhally 1987). In Baudrillard's (1988) account, use-value becomes a subordinated part of exchange value under the auspices of the 'commodity-sign'. The 'sign' component is crucial, as signs are autonomous from material commodities and this produces advertising with almost limitless scope to mark objects with new associations. It is these new semantic associations rather than material characteristics that drive consumption in contemporary society.

This search for meaning through consumption is the defining feature of consumer society. As Baudrillard suggests:

> If we consume the product as product, we consume its meaning through advertising. [. . .] We make believe that products are so differentiated and multiplied that they have become complex things and consequently purchasing and consumption must have the same value as any social relation.
>
> (Baudrillard, 1988: 10, 14)

This is an important point. The '*cultural*' consumer society succeeds prior '*social*' forms of society as a direct result of the change in the economic system of production. Baudrillard's ideas on this matter have had a major influence on critical thinking about advertising. Wernick (1991: 16–18) reworks and elaborates these notions in a more detailed account of the operation of 'promotional culture'. For Wernick, industrialization heralded 'artificial semiosis' or the industrial manufacture of 'commodity-signs' whereby advertising 're-codes' products with psycho-cultural appeal. The result, once more, is the devaluing of 'authentic culture' and ultimately, for Wernick, the dissolution of the boundaries between the economic regime of accumulation and the cultural regime of signification. Similar concerns appear in Leiss *et al.*'s (1990) account of advertising as the 'bridge' between production and consumption that has come to define the 'cultural frame for goods'. They echo the critical trend in which consumer societies play host to a profound transformation of the culture/economy relation occasioned by the combined effects of industrialization, mass production and accelerated technological innovation. Underlying this is a sense of culture and economy, outside of commodity systems of production, as separate and bounded domains of activity.

This idea carries enormous critical weight and attempts to reformulate the culture/economy relationship have been ongoing in recent decades. Harvey (1989) and Jameson (1991) developed the Frankfurt school and post-Althusserian tradition of analysis to provide an account of the ways in which culture in the late twentieth century has increasingly been colonized by the economic imperatives of capitalist modes of production. In another branch of theoretical work, the relation is reformulated such that influence runs in the opposite direction from the cultural to the economic as cultural knowledges gain precedence in the system of production. This is the version of culture and economy presented in Lash and Urry's (1987, 1994) analyses. In their terms the contemporary or 'disorganized' phase of capitalism has witnessed the erosion of the boundaries between economic and cultural processes (1994: 64). A number of forces, from growth in the prominence of 'culture industries' and cultural goods to the increasing role of 'signifying practices' in different forms of work, are implicated in this transition but the role of advertising is of particular significance. For Lash and Urry, advertising acts as a crucial enabling technology in the transition from one mode of societal organization to the next (1987: 293). It is central to the dominance of consumption widely regarded as definitive of the 'post-industrial' society. Advertising is precisely the sort of institution which in merging economic objectives with cultural knowledges acts to combine the economic 'system' with the cultural 'environment' in new ways (Lash and Urry, 1994: 64). In many respects, advertising practitioners exemplify this trend in that they are explicitly engaged in the symbolic work of producing needs. This aspect of Lash and Urry's account draws upon Bourdieu's formulation of the structural positioning of the new fraction of the petit bourgeoisie he described as 'cultural intermediaries'. These are: 'new or renovated positions [that] result from recent changes in the economy (in particular, the increasing role of the symbolic work of producing needs, even in the production of goods- design, packaging, sales promotion, marketing, advertising etc.)' (Bourdieu, 1984: 345). Of particular note here is Bourdieu's attribution of this new structural position to recent economic changes. Bourdieu saw the juxtaposition of symbolic practices with economic knowledges as a new departure related to a much broader set of changes in the economic organization of 'post' industrialized societies. In this he was clearly not alone. Over the last two decades a growing number of theorists have been concerned with the ways in which cultural intermediary occupations exemplify substantive changes in the nature of the relation between the once 'sealed-off' domains of culture and economy (Featherstone, 1991; Mort, 1996; Nixon, 1996, 1997; du Gay, et al., 1997). This has been accompanied by a growing interest in the nature of cultural intermediary types of work and it is this that has provided the impetus for critical work focused on advertising *practice* rather than *texts*.

Amongst its major contributions to the critical debate on advertising the 'practice-based literature' effectively problematized some of the main claims made about advertising in text-based analyses (Moeran, 1996; Mort, 1996; Nixon, 1996; Miller, 1997). Practice-based literature clearly established the uncomfortable disjuncture between the working universe of practitioners concerned with routine problems of sales curves, failing campaigns and the difficulties of integrating advertising campaigns with broader business strategies and critical accounts of the subtle ideological manipulation of subjects. Notwithstanding these gains, the close attention to contemporary practices also carried with it one unanticipated cost. In throwing light upon the nature, characteristics and values of advertising practitioners as an occupational group, the literature also got caught up in an overstatement of the epochal, emblematic significance of this group.

Soar (1997: 13), for example, describes advertising creatives as 'cultural intermediaries', who constitute both a 'class fraction' and a 'taste culture' and are made up of mainly young, mainly metropolitan, well-educated and well-resourced individuals. According to Thornton (1999: 63), creatives not only conform to these criteria but adopt quite distinctive standards of behaviour.

> Creatives are not supposed to wear business attire . . . This might under-
> mine their claims to creativity. For example . . . when the chairman rec-
> ommended that staff refrained from wearing jeans or shorts . . . a good
> proportion of the creative department came in wearing shorts, some of
> them obscenely short. What would have been seen as childish behaviour in
> others was not only seen as acceptable but as reassuring evidence of the
> 'creativity' of creatives.
>
> (1999: 63)

Mort (1996) has described how this sort of identity position is regarded in the industry as central to the creative function. Creatives, in order to meet their organizational brief, *had* to adopt lifestyles and modes of behaviour quite separate from 'stiff business culture' (1996: 101). These patterns of behaviour are seen as necessary to enable creatives to perform as 'cognoscenti' who can provide taste leadership (Mort, 1996: 96). In a similar vein, Soar remarks on creatives' 'very considerable appetite for all that is new in film, television, radio, magazines, products and services' (1996: 30). Creatives emerge here as cultural intermedi-aries who use their own experiences to construct imagery and form opinion.

Crucially, as in Bourdieu's formulation, these cultural intermediaries are seen in the practice-based literature as a new fraction responding to 'broad-based economic and cultural change' (Mort, 1996: 93). The 1980s were widely charac-terized within the advertising industry as an 'age of creativity'. This new emphasis on the creative was articulated around shifts towards more aesthetic, image-driven, artistic and emotional advertising. Both Mort (1996: 1–12) and Nixon (1997: 186–8) are keen to avoid the critical tendency – evident in Baudrillard and Wernick's work – towards over-abstraction and over-generalization of 'epochal' shifts towards a consumer society. Mort (1996: 4), for instance, situates his particularist concerns against theoretical formulations of the consumer revol-ution that understand 'contemporary shifts as epochal and totalizing, breaking with what had gone before'. Yet, despite his desire to avoid such hyperbolic claims, Mort maintains that the 'creative' concept:

> . . . did dramatise a set of more concrete changes underway within the
> advertising and marketing industries in the 1980s. As the third wave
> agencies saw it, the core problem confronting the whole profession was the
> massive increase in the levels of material provision since the Second World
> War. . . . Traditional messages of social improvement or price competi-
> tiveness, needed to be replaced by an approach which was more in tune
> with the demands of a generation of advanced customers. Today's adver-
> tiser's needed to suggest philosophies of living and styles of behaviour,
> rather than simply pushing the product.
>
> (1996: 97)

Similarly Nixon (1996: 76) asserts that the 'creative revolution' reconfigured the priorities of advertising, altering ideas about effectiveness and how the consumer should be addressed. Changes in creative priorities, he explains, were reinforced by parallel changes in account planning and media buying practices that fed a move towards creative advertisements structured around an 'Emotional Selling Point' (ESP).[1] ESP ads were 'image led' and characterized by specific representational techniques encompassing particular filming, editing and lighting methods.

The view that changes in advertising's appearance and content from reason and information to emotion and persuasion are symptomatic of its evolution in tandem with broader, epochal patterns of social and economic change has an almost axiomatic status in critical theory (Williams, 1980; Dyer, 1982; Pope, 1983; Leiss et al., 1990; Falk, 1994; Fowles, 1996). In many respects, whilst the claims of writers like Mort and Nixon are circumscribed, their emphasis on the 'emotional' third wave in advertising agencies as a response to post-war conditions of plenty implies a similar logic. This logic is one in which advertising practice moves towards the increasing utilization of aesthetic, style-based *cultural* knowledges in order to pursue its instrumental, *economic* aims more effectively.

Characterizations of advertising in this vein share a sense of underlying structural change. If advertising is becoming more of a culture industry, if its practitioners are becoming more like cultural intermediaries this is in some way related to broader changes in the configuration of culture and economy in the late twentieth century. In this sense these discussions of advertising practice feature a sort of teleological undercurrent that sees in industry practices a unique hybridity of culture and economy. There is a problem, however, with these arguments about the distinctiveness of contemporary advertising in that their description of historical specificity derives from a past that is largely assumed rather than known. To theorize about ruptures, transgressions and mutations in culture and economy is logically to invoke a different past but, as shall be seen in the next section, some significant details of that past have been largely overlooked by critical theory.

Pioneers and precursors: the first advertising creatives

> Too many copy writers think in terms of big places like New York and of cultured people of the sort with which they associate and too little about simple people who after all make up the great masses.
>
> (Charles Hoyt agency training manual, 1926, HOYTa)

> [A]n in-house survey of New York copywriters conducted for J. Walter Thompson in 1936 . . . found that not one copywriter belonged to a lodge or civic club; only one in five went to church except on rare occasions; half

never went to Coney Island or any other popular public resort and the others only once or twice a year; more than half had never lived within the national average income of $1580 per year, and half did not know anyone who ever had. While 5 percent of American homes had servants, 66 percent of J. Walter Thompson homes did. The profile was affluent, metropolitan, secular and (superficially) sophisticated, and this was typical of the most prominent agencies with the largest accounts.

(Lears, 1994: 197)

What the above comments immediately suggest is something of the atypicality of advertising producers even at the start of this century. This atypically is not the only characteristic that the early producers of advertising share with their contemporary equivalent. In his discussion of the role of this new class of specialists in symbolic production, Featherstone (1991: 43–7) argues that their particular mix of emotional, aesthetic and stylistic sensitivities can be traced back to the Romantic movement of the early nineteenth century. What is new for Featherstone is not the existence of these attributes *per se* but their extent, proliferation and clustering around new occupational groupings particularly in advertising, marketing, media and the arts. These symbolic occupations are widely understood to have increased both numerically and in the power and influence they command in society in the second half of the twentieth century (Featherstone, 1991; Wernick, 1991; Lash and Urry, 1994).

This emphasis on numeric proliferation is problematic. Enormous difficulties apply to the task of assessing the *relative* numeric significance of people defined as working in symbolic or cultural occupations over the last 300 years.[2] Furthermore, even where such statistical puzzles are satisfactorily addressed one conceptual dilemma will inevitably remain – the cultural and economic universes of the eighteenth, nineteenth and twentieth centuries are fundamentally dissimilar entities. In this respect, it can never be a simple matter to claim that social experience, *as a whole*, at any one historical moment is more cultural, more hybridized or more economic than at another. Rather than attempting to define some objective means of comparing the concentration of cultural influences in commercial practice over the last few centuries, the approach taken here is to consider how cultural and economic elements were unavoidably combined in the work and lives of early advertising producers.

One early indication of this may be surmised from the fragments of evidence that remain about the lives of key groups of people who circulated around the earliest advertising agencies. Whilst their precise nature and early functions may be a matter of some debate, the first advertising agents can be fairy reliably traced to the beginning of the nineteenth century.[3] One of these, RF White, an agency which survived in one form or another into the 1980s, was founded in 1800 by James White. White was a writer and a key player in London's literary scene. He was a friend of the essayist Charles Lamb and there are a number of references in Lamb's correspondence to attempts to promote White's book (RFW 2/3 Whites Box HATa). Lamb himself also had occasional involvement in advertising production as his sister May wrote in 1809: 'White has prevailed upon him to write some more lottery puffs' (RFW 1/6/1 Whites Box HATa).

Links between early advertising agencies and the literary and artistic circles of nineteenth-century London also emerge in the life of Thomas Alsager. Alsager was city correspondent of *The Times* from 1817 but in the very different institutional arrangements of the period this involved his being situated at the offices of Lawson and Barker. Lawson and Barker were founded in 1812 and later became the advertising agency, Charles Barker. At this stage, however, the firm were carrying out a variety of different operations including city and parliamentary news gathering, overseas and provincial news and newspaper distribution as well as placing advertisements in *The Times* and a variety of other newspapers (Letters Book 1825–1847 MS 20011, CBa). Alsager's life and connections are relatively well documented in *The History of The Times Vol. 1*:

> He was versatile and held a prominent position in two arts: finance and music . . . he was a frequent visitor to Leigh Hunt during his imprisonment. Hunt had much affection for him and dedicated a sonnet to his name . . . Lamb was fond of him and chronicles his sayings and doings in letters to their friend Wordsworth. . . . On December 24th, 1832, Beethoven's Mass in D was given at Alsager's for the first time in England.
>
> (n.d.: 415)

This is suggestive of the types of social milieu some early figures in advertising existed in. It is of some significance that Charles Lamb had connections to both Whites and Barkers, which were amongst only a handful of agencies in operation at the time. In addition, White was a contact of Josiah Wedgewood and the poet Robert Southey (Crowsley, c. 1951, Whites Box, HATa; Stuart, 1889). These connections are unremarkable when viewed in the context of the much less clearly demarcated relations that existed at the time between agencies, manufacturers and newspapers.

Newspapers like *The Times* and Daniel Stuart's *Morning Post* had extremely close connections to advertising institutions. *The Times* was linked to Barkers and another firm, Streets. By the early 1800s Streets were hiring out copies of *The Times* and acting as an advertising broker to it and other newspapers (Chipchase, Streets file, HATa). The range of activities that these early agencies were involved in frequently embraced literary work, publishing, the book trade, journalism and news agency. This network is of some consequence because it undoubtedly patterned the lives and conducts of early practitioners.

This can be gleaned from letters published in the *Gentlemen's Magazine* between June and August 1838 regarding the relationship between Stuart, the proprietor of the *Morning Post*, and the poet Samuel Coleridge. These letters refer to Coleridge's claim that his 'literary department' – comprising Robert Southey, William Wordsworth and Charles Lamb – had made the fortune of the paper but had received scant financial reward for it. Stuart refuted this claim, arguing that Coleridge exaggerated his and his fellow writers contributions; the fortune of the paper, according to Stuart, owed more to its policy of attracting 'numerous and varied' advertisements (July, 1838). Regardless of whether Coleridge or Stuart's version of events is preferred, what the lengthy exchange on the matter does make clear is the extent of connections both socially and occupationally between writers like Coleridge, newspaper proprietors like Stuart and advertisers like Wedgewood and Christie the auctioneer.

These connections emerge in other correspondence between Southey, Wordsworth, Coleridge and Stuart (Stuart, 1889). When Coleridge set up his own periodical, *The Friend*, he produced 'rude sketches of short advertisements' for Stuart to check and place in *The Morning Post* (Stuart, 1889: 450). Southey also refers to the importance of advertising in another letter to Stuart: 'One newspaper will do more for a book than two reviews. I thank you for the lift you have given *Esprilla*, and will write to make Longman follow it up by advertising which they certainly do not do enough' (Southey to Stuart, November 27 1807, in *Ibid.*).

There were, then, close links between early advertising practitioners and the book trade. This was a matter of some concern to critics like Macaulay (1830) and the pseudonymous author Master Trimmer (1826) who lamented the links between literary circles, advertising and publishing. Book reviews according to the latter were 'nothing now but vehicles for the puffing of trash books' (Stuart, 1889: 4). For Macaulay the 'shameful' artifice of book advertising had become so widespread by the 1820s that it was endangering the literary character (1830: 196). Macaulay's irritation was not simply with the dignity of puffing. At least as important was the convoluted network of interests which linked authors, book publishers and periodical publishers and enabled their 'despicable ingenuity' (Stuart, 1889: 196).

> The publisher is often the publisher of some periodical work. In this periodical the first flourish of trumpets is sounded. The peal is then echoed and re-echoed by all the other periodical works over which the publisher or the author, or the author's coterie has any influence. The newspapers are for a fortnight filled with puffs or all the various kinds which Sheridan recounted, – direct, oblique and collusive.
>
> (1830: 197)

These connections between advertising, the press and the book trade led to the construction of an elaborate promotional machine where the notoriety of authors could be carefully constructed and managed in what would appear to be an independent editorial (cf. Macaulay, 1830). Moreover, this extension of editorial puffing into a system of hype has to be understood as simultaneously the product of the publisher's economic calculations *and* their immersion in a journalistic mode of cultural production.

This was a very different field of production than that typical of contemporary advertising. The organization of advertising production was much less tightly defined or specialized than it was to become. Whilst precisely who did what is likely to remain obscure, it is highly probable that in spite of the arrival on the scene of the first advertising agencies whoever considered themselves to have an interest in producing advertising continued to do so. In this respect, retailers, manufacturers, entrepreneurs, publishers, journalists and other writers all contributed to advertising and in doing so imported specific repertoires of knowledge and specific commercial objectives.

Many of the people who had an involvement in advertising production in this period also had recognizable forms of aesthetic knowledge. Although the exact division of labour is unknown it is clear that the staff of agencies like Barkers and Whites had connections to literary, artistic and musical circles while artistic figures like Lamb, Southey and Coleridge were involved in some way in the production of advertising. These sorts of aesthetic competencies and connections continued to be important and became the subject of more formal mechanisms for development amongst the specialist creatives employed in the developing 'full service' advertising agency of the late nineteenth century. 'Full service' was the term used to describe firms who had begun to extend their provision to include more formalized creative and planning services. Such agencies began to employ artists and copywriters towards the end of the nineteenth century, although their use did not become widespread throughout the industry until the 1910s to 1920s. As their occupational roles became more established, certain features both in the type of practices employed and the type of people who would be recruited began to emerge.

One creative practice that emerged early was the pooling of ideas and images for copy and layout. Hower (1939) describes how the Ayer agency in the 1890s began to run competitions to generate more ideas for copy and systematically built up collections of copy. From the 1890s onwards agencies like Sell's, Benson's, Crawfords, JWT and Ayer kept scrapbooks or guardbooks. These books were often used to record advertisements and campaigns produced internally and any press coverage of agency work. Ashley Havinden, an illustrator who worked for Crawfords from 1921 kept scrapbooks of 'sticker labels, brochures and magazine ads, mostly German- and Bauhaus-inclined' (Feaver, 1975: 76). Most agencies kept advertisements for competing products as well as their own. JWT's archive contains many samples of competitors' advertising and the account files bear witness to the material import of this work in situating new campaigns. In this sense, these early creatives, like those in the contemporary industry, worked with their eyes closely fixed both on the competition and on the broader artistic community.

The importance for creatives to have both an understanding of commercial priorities and a developed aesthetic repertoire was recognized quite early in some agencies. JWT, Ayer and Calkins and Holden in the USA (Lears, 1994; Bogart, 1995) and Crawfords, Sells and Bensons in the UK made systematic efforts to engineer and maintain links to external artistic communities. Earnest Elmo Calkins of Calkins and Holden, for example, campaigned to improve the artistic standards of advertising and hosted a series of exhibitions promoting art in advertising (Bogart, 1995). In JWT, newsletters from the 1920s and 1930s reviewed current art exhibits and would feature articles from commissioned artists and photographers like Edward Steichen (JWTa). The firm also ran its own internal gallery, as did Ayer in the same period. In 1927, art directors Ross Shattuck of JWT and Charles Coiner of Ayer held a joint exhibition of their paintings (Lears, 1994). The emerging sense of the occupational milieu of creatives at least in these agencies is one of immersion in a very particular taste culture, as the following description of Paul Darrow's experiences in Ayer's art department in the 1920s and 1930s illustrates:

> From the beginning Ayer was a stimulating place to work. What was the mystique? I am sure to a large part it was the people with whom I worked. Real published authors in the copy department. Granville Toogood from an old Philadelphia family who was as interested in black jazz as I was – and got me on the list of Rittenhouse Square's favourite bootlegger. Dick Powell, Mark Goodrich, Jerry Mangione, John Pullen and Charlie Fisher who had studied cooking while on the Paris trip taught me to make a real French omelette. In the art department Paul Froelich, some of whose rich watercolours for Switzerland Cheese, Fostoria etc. had first lured me to Ayer. Leon Karp who taught me a great deal about painting and the real meaning of the French Impressionists.
>
> (Paul Darrow, n.d. AYERa)

These links were also reflected in the policies of agencies like Ayer and JWT towards commissioning established artists to produce advertising. Such policies had precedents in English and French poster advertising in the nineteenth century, which had featured work by artists like Millais, Frith, Beardsley, Cheret and Lautrec. Ayer in the 1920s to 1940s was one of the foremost in this respect and commissioned freelance advertising work from artists like Salvador Dali, Andre Derain, Raoul Duffy, Marie Lawrencin, Pablo Picasso, Pierre Roy and Ignacio (Clarence Jordan memoirs, AYERa).

Some of these advertising commissions were from the realm of what Bourdieu might label 'legitimate culture' (1984) or what Horkheimer and Adorno (1979) might call 'serious, autonomous' art. Their presence in advertising is an indication of the complicated relations that exist between advertising, art worlds and commercial practices. At one level advertising practitioners sought to legitimate advertising with 'legitimate' art. At another level art was an intrinsic element in the everyday work of people like Ayer's art director Paul Darrow. At the operational level, artistic and commercial motivations coexisted in the decision to use particular types of artwork. In practice, the choice of a specific artist often grew out of working practices and connections and was closely articulated to the commercial aims of the campaign.

Figure 1, for instance, shows an advertising photograph by Edward Steichen for JWT's Jergen's lotion account. The design was one of the first 'realist'

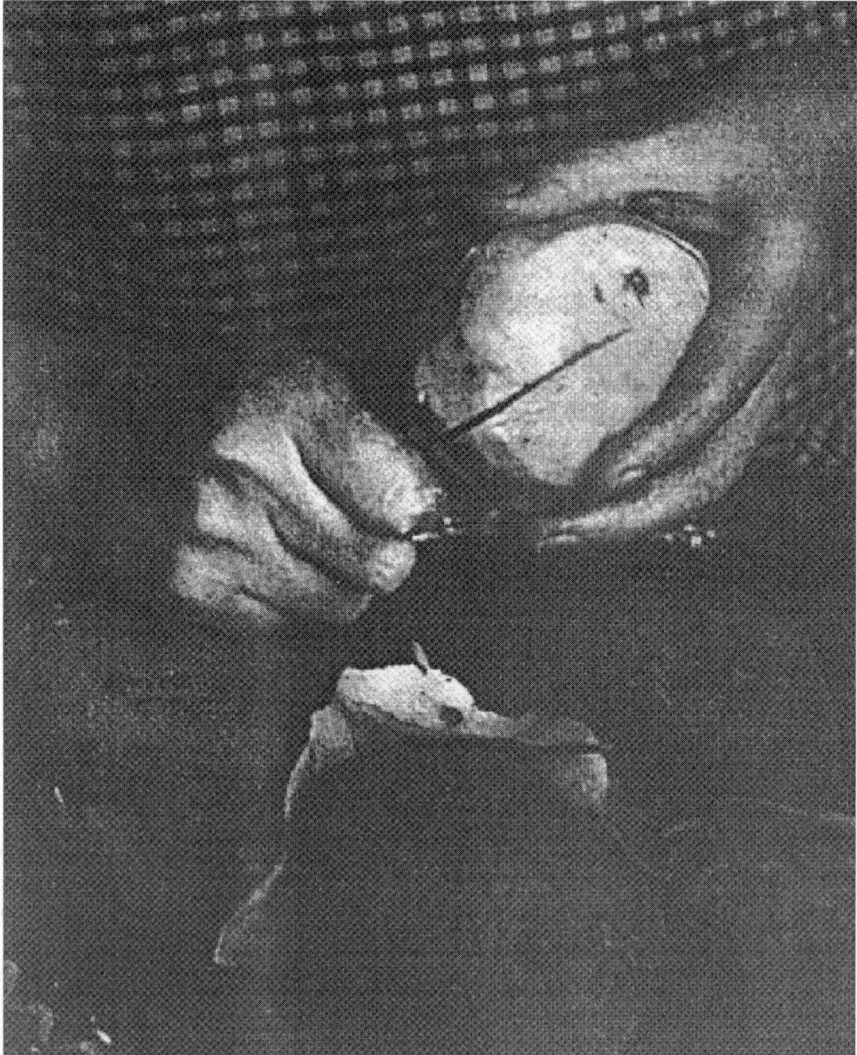

Figure 1 Edward Steichen's work for Jergen's Lotion (Source: Steichen, 1962).

photographs used in an advertising campaign and Steichen was already a well known photographer/artist by the time it was commissioned (Steichen, 1962). The decision to use this style of photography was closely linked to a marketing decision to resituate the lotion as a product for care of the hands. This was a decision that was itself rooted in other contextual factors. The market for facial skin care – the 'complexion' as advertisers redefined it around this time – had been successfully captured by companies like Pond's. Jergen's therefore needed to 'redefine' their product and its market. A 1923 market research investigation suggested some consumers preferred to use the lotion on the hands and this led JWT to identify a new market 'women of the middle class who do their own housework' (Account Files, Box 1, JWTa). The choice of Edward Steichen was calculated as a way of getting this new message across through using 'sincere, dramatic and beautiful' photographs of familiar tasks (Account Files, Box 1, JWTa). What the Jergen's lotion campaign illustrates is how closely artistic and commercial aspirations were interweaved. Steichen's willingness to take on the commission was a function of the level of reimbursement and dissemination it afforded. JWT's decision to use Steichen reflected the opinion that the dramatic impact of this photography would be an effective commercial tool to reposition the product.

If advertising art was closely linked to external art worlds, parallel links were also in play between advertising copy and external literary culture. The stereotype of the copywriter with unrequited literary ambitions arose for good reason. The files of agencies are full of staff who went on to publish novels, poetry and biography. Dorothy Sayers worked for the agency Benson's in the 1920s in a copy department known at the time as the 'literary room' – a term also favoured by US agencies like Charles Austin Bates and Ayer. The privileged role of literary influences in Ayer also emerges in Weir's recollection of the management of copywriting:

> Fry never interfered with Copy in any way. You had a free hand and he saw to it that people were recruited for the dept. who were not just copywriters who had done well in another agency but people who had written books, plays. He got genuine writers . . . poets . . . Jim Daley, Granny Toogood . . . many others.
>
> (Walter Weir: Ayer copywriter 1928–34, AYERa)

As agencies began to move away from using freelance writers in preference to employing in-house copywriters, they made frequent references to the status of copywriting as a specialist type of writing. Numerous treatises were published on how to write advertising and 'star' copywriters like JWT's James Webb Young and Helen Lansdowne Resor, Benson's Oswald Greene and Dorothy Sayers and Ayer's Granville Toogood began to emerge. In an article on the challenge of copywriting, JWT used Aldous Huxley's description of advertisements as 'one of the most interesting and difficult of modern literary forms' (JWT Junior Newsletter, February 1936). This specialism in large part was considered to arise from the need to combine literary skills with commercial objectives in a limited amount of space. Copywriters had to consider: 'the amount of space needed to tell the story, the positions of copy, the kind of headline, the prominence of logotype, the appeal the copy should carry for breaking down resistance or building up active demand' (JWT Junior Newsletter, February 1936).

In these respects the creative work of the first specialist copywriters and art directors might be defined as *constituent* practices in that they seem, necessarily, to combine cultural and economic knowledges.

The point to be drawn from this evidence is that, in many crucial respects, the historical producers of advertising could reasonably qualify as cultural intermediaries. In the early nineteenth century there were clear occupational links between those involved in the production of advertising and literary, newspaper and publishing circles. These links appear to have been of material significance in shaping advertising forms and styles. By the early twentieth century links between advertising practitioners and literary and artistic circles can be more systematically documented. By this point formal mechanisms existed in some agencies to foster and develop aesthetic competence to facilitate the production of effective advertising. In terms of lifestyles, connections and competencies then, there would appear to be close parallels between these early practitioners and recent descriptions of late twentieth-century creative staff.

So what about the old cultural intermediaries?

> Consumer culture is always 'new', but there has been a different more consequential kind of newness in the air over the past few decades, a sense of structural transformation within modernity itself, of ruptures in its economic, social and cultural modes of carrying on. This sense of an epochal shift has been the focus of most social theory . . .
>
> (Slater, 1997: 174)

If some of the earliest producers of advertising meet many of the defining criteria of 'new cultural intermediaries', this raises two quite different but closely related sorts of questions about the utility of the term. The first concerns the emphasis on the *new* and the second concerns the notion of *intermediary* and the aim in this concluding section is to briefly consider both of these in turn.

As Slater's comments above indicate, much social theory has been concerned with a 'more consequential kind of newness' and this concern can be traced in recent literature focused on the practice of advertising. While this literature provides an important and overdue release from the dominance of textual approaches, it has been caught up in the critical preoccupation with defining the precise nature of the epoch and the place occupied by advertising within it. This preoccupation can be traced in the characterization of the cultural intermediary. The advertising practitioner as cultural intermediary has been conceptualized as one element in a sweeping process of structural transformation in which the culture/economy relation is central. In this, the advertising practitioner has become emblematic of the transfer of culture into the economic realm. Now most theorists would concede that this transfer is precedented; as both Feather-stone (1991) and Nixon (1996) have acknowledged, there is nothing particularly new in the use of aesthetic knowledges to attain commercial goals. What the evidence presented here begins to suggest, however, is that the historical relation between the aesthetic or 'cultural' and the economic runs much deeper than the occasional use of art or literature in advertising.

Although much discussion of cultural intermediaries has tended to use the terms 'aesthetic', 'symbolic' and 'cultural' almost interchangeably, it is import-ant at this point to distinguish between these terms. The aesthetic might be used to refer to all those aspects of an individual's skills, knowledges and personal comportment relating to the arts, literature, music and fashion. The 'cultural' on the other hand it is often used to invoke this aesthetic realm *and* any other prac-tices relating to signification and the production of meaning. The historical evidence clearly suggests that there were calculated attempts to import aesthetic competences into the production of advertising. But, it was not only groups like writers and artists, with discernible aesthetic competencies, who brought 'culture' into advertising – so too did the journalists, and book and newspaper publishers. All these groups of people substantively influenced the form of adver-tising by introducing new and distinctive sets of meanings, values and knowledges to the process. This signals some difficulties with the idea of the intermediary as a *new* structural position but, more importantly, it also raises questions about the concept of the 'intermediary'.

The whole notion of intermediary status presupposes a conceptualization of culture and economy as separate and bounded domains. Whether the distinc-tiveness of the contemporary moment resides in the Frankfurt school vision of culture entirely subordinated to economy or in a later 'post-Fordist' view of culture as organizing the economy, it is clear that culture and economy are supposed to be separate. This type of thinking is undoubtedly convenient from an analytical viewpoint, it is much easier to think about all aspects of social life if these categories are kept discrete. But the broader 'cultural' input, the specific sets of meanings and values that the various occupational groups brought to the advertising process are extremely difficult to disentangle from its economic dimensions. The problem of separating the cultural from the economic has been remarked upon by numerous authors concerned with the detailed study of material, social practices.

Anthropologists like Sahlins (1976), Appadurai (1986) and Miller (1997), for instance, have argued that in practice the 'cultural' and the 'economic' are always interlinked. Material or economic forces here cannot be understood to determine culture because the two are structurally interdependent. For these authors, economic practices are culturally defined whilst cultural meanings are shared and disseminated through economic activities in any recorded society. This way of thinking about culture and economy is given another twist in Turner's (1992) analysis of Max Weber's work. In his terms:

> As long as we talk of the relationship between culture 'and' politics, culture 'and' economics, between a realm of culture which pertains to human inwardness and a social realm which does not, we will miss the point completely. 'Culture' *is not a sphere at all.*
>
> (1992: 43)

What Turner is getting at is Weber's much less restrictive definition of culture, which rather than opposing culture to other 'spheres' of existence whether 'economic', 'social' or 'political' sees culture as constitutive of all value-spheres. For some writers (Sayer, 1994; Grossberg, 1998), this encompassing view equates culture with human experience and risks dissolving the distinctiveness of the term. But such concerns about the dissolution of culture grant it a sort of bounded, ahistorical reality that overlooks just how local and historically specific the notion of culture as a separate and bounded sphere is. Williams' (1976) discussion highlighted how recent and multifaceted contemporary usages of the term culture are. The general notion of culture as referring to processes of human development and civilization only began to appear during the Enlightenment whilst the specific association of culture with higher arts, philosophy and learning did not emerge until the late nineteenth century (du Gay, *et al.*, 1997).

Yet if culture is defined as constitutive of all meaningful activities, this raises questions about exactly how it is to be distinguished from the economic realm. It is not as if the economic could exist without the mediation of human values and meanings. In this sense, culture is not something that intervenes in economic processes, rather it is *constitutive* of them. For this reason the approach located here is to leave the precise definition of what in practice is cultural and what is economic behind to focus instead on a *constituent view of practice*. This is intended to invoke a sense of the impossibility of the purely economic or the purely cultural. In practice, as authors like Callon (1998) and Law (2000) have argued, the domains of culture and economy are not ahistorical realities but the results of specific processes of configuration. As Law (2000) put it:

> culture doesn't exist in the abstract . . . Instead, or in addition, culture is located and performed in human and non-human material practices. And these are material practices which extend beyond and implicate not only human beings, subjects and their meanings but also technical, architectural, geographical and corporeal arrangements.
>
> (2000: 2)

Law's remarks are useful because they highlight how culture extends to cover not simply human meanings, as it is widely characterized in critique, but also encompasses material arrangements. This view of culture has been developed in parallel discussions of the ways in which economics acts to shape, format or 'perform' the economy (Callon, 1998). In Callon's analysis the economy does not exist in the abstract as a 'thing' awaiting study and analysis by economists. Rather it is the contingent outcome of a process of configuration in which economics and the economy move together in a mutual 'performation'. The economy exists but not in a 'natural' state, rather its existence is formatted and framed by economics (1998: 51). Underlying all this work is a sort of base-line commitment to the notion that 'culture' and 'economy' exist only in relation to material practice. This conceptualization makes the precise separation of the economic from the cultural a bit redundant. Together both dimensions constitute practice.

The historical evidence presented, together with theoretical debates about the nature of culture and economy, suggests that the notion of the contemporary advertising practitioner as a new cultural intermediary should be approached with some caution. Whilst the fragmentary nature of the evidence makes it difficult to assert much with any degree of certainty, there would appear nevertheless to be very clear parallels between some early practitioners and Bourdieu's (1984) new cultural intermediaries. Further, from a theoretical viewpoint, it is clear that the validity of the notion of the intermediary depends entirely upon an acceptance of culture and economy as normatively separate domains. What recent reappraisal of the terms has done is to highlight that this separation is based more on intellectual habit than substantive evidence.

Notes

1   The notion of ESP stands in opposition to the 'traditional' Unique Selling Proposition (USP) approach described in Rosser Reeves (1961) 'Reality in Advertising', where ads seek to stress a 'unique' feature of each product.

2   Unsurprisingly, statistical information in direct support of this view is comparatively rare. Such surveys as are available tend to address much more tightly delimited questions such as the rise in particular occupational groups, e.g. the service class (see Lash and Urry, 1987) in the post-war period.

3   Against the view dating the first 'proper' agencies to the late nineteenth century (Turner, 1952; Pope 1983; Leiss et al., 1990; Lears, 1994), Terry Nevett (1977) and Paul Chipchase (1977, HATa) identify Tayler and Newton in 1786 as the first followed by Whites (1800), Reynells (1812), Charles Barker (1812) and Deacons (1812) on the basis of evidence derived from London trade directories.

References

Appadurai, Arjun (1986) *The Social Life of Things*. Cambridge: Cambridge University Press.

Baudrillard, Jean (1988) 'Consumer Society', in Mark Poster (ed.) *Selected Writings*. Cambridge: Polity Press.

Bogart, Michele (1995) *Artists, Advertising and the Borders of Art*. Chicago: University of Chicago Press.

Bourdieu, Pierre (1984) *Distinction: A Critique of the Judgement of Taste*. London: Routledge.

Callon, M. (1998) 'Introduction: the embeddedness of economic markets in economics', in M. Callon (ed.) *The Laws of the Markets*. Oxford: Blackwell.

Du Gay, Paul, Hall, Stuart, Janes, Linda, Mackay, Hugh and Negus, Keith (1997) *Doing Cultural Studies: the Story of the Sony Walkman*. London: Sage.

Dyer, Gillian (1982) *Advertising as Communication*. London: Routledge.

Falk, Pasi (1994) *The Consuming Body*. London: Sage.

Featherstone, Michael (1991) *Consumer Culture and Postmodernism*. London: Sage.

Feaver, William (1975) 'Walk the Ashley way'. *Sunday Times Colour Magazine*, 13 April.

Fowles, Jib (1996) *Advertising and Popular Culture*. London: Sage.

Grossberg, Lawrence (1998) 'Cultural studies crossroads blues'. *European Journal of Cultural Studies*, 1(1).

Harvey, David (1989) *The Condition of Postmodernity*. Oxford: Blackwell.

Haug, Wolfgang (1986) *Critique of Commodity Aesthetics*. London: Polity.

Horkheimer, Max and Adorno, Theodore (1979/1947) *Dialectic of Enlightenment*. London: Verso.

Jameson, Frederick (1991) 'Postmodernism or the cultural logic of late capitalism'. *New Left Review*, 146: 55–92.

Jhally, Sut (1987) *The Codes of Advertising: Fetishism and the Political Economy of Meaning in Consumer Society*. London: Routledge.

Lash, Scott and Urry, John (1987) *The End of Organised Capitalism*. Cambridge: Polity.

Lash, Scott and Urry, John (1994) *Economies of Signs and Space*. London: Sage.

Law, J. (2001) 'Economics as interference', in P. du Gay and M. Pryke (eds) *Cultural Economy: Cultural Analysis and Commercial Life*. London: Sage.

Lears, Jackson (1994). *Fables of Abundance: a Cultural History of Advertising in America*. New York: Basic Books.

Leiss, William *et al.* (1990) *Social Communication In Advertising*. London: Routledge.

Macaulay (1830) 'Mr Robert Montgomery's poems and the modern practice of puffing'. *Edinburgh Review*, April, ci: 194–210.

Miller, Daniel (1997) *Capitalism: an Ethnographic Approach*. London: Berg.

Moeran, Brian (1996) *A Japanese Advertising Agency*. Surrey: Curzon.

Mort, Frank (1996) *Cultures of Consumption*. London: Routledge.

Nevett, Terry (1977) 'London's early advertising agents'. *Journal of Advertising History*, 1, December: 15–18.

Nixon, Sean (1996) *Hard Looks: Masculinities, Spectatorship and Contemporary Consumption*. London: UCL Press Ltd.

—— (1997) 'Circulating culture', in P. du Gay (ed.) *Production of Culture/Cultures of Production*. London: Sage.

Pope, Daniel (1983) *The Making of Modern Advertising*. New York: Basic Books.

Presbrey, Frank (1929) *The History and Development of Advertising*. New York: Greenwood.

Sahlins, Marshall (1976) *Culture and Practical Reason*. Chicago: University of Chicago Press.

Sayer, Andrew (1996) 'Cultural studies and the "economy"'. *Environment and Planning: Society and Space*, 12: 635–637.

Slater, Don (1997) *Consumer Culture and Modernity*. Cambridge: Polity.

Steichen, Edward (1962) *My Life in Photography*. New York: Doubleday.

Stuart, Rosemary (compiler) (1889) *Letters from the Lake Poets to Daniel Stuart*. London. *The History of The Times*, Vol. 1, n.d.

Thornton, Sarah (1999) 'An academic Alice in Adland; ethnography and the commercial world'. *Critical Quarterly*, 4(1).

Trimmer, Master (1826) *Siege of Pater Noster Row: A Moral Satire*. London.

Turner, Charles (1992) *Modernity and Politics in the Work of Max Weber*. London: Routledge.

Turner, E. S. (1952) *The Shading History of Advertising*. London: Michael Joseph.

Wernick, Andrew (1991) *Promotional Culture: Advertising, Ideology and Symbolic Expression*. London: Sage.

Williams, Raymond (1980) 'Advertising, the magic system'. *Problems in Materialism and Culture*. London: Verso.

—— (1976) *Keywords*. London: Fontana.

Williamson, Judith (1978) *Decoding Advertisements*. London: Marion Boyars.

Unpublished sources

Conference and seminar papers and dissertations

Slater, Don (2000) 'Capturing Markets from the Economists'. Paper given at the *Culture Economy Workshop*, Open University, 13–14 January.

Soar, Matthew (1997) The children of Marx and Coca-cola: advertising and commercial creativity. Unpublished MA thesis, Simon Fraser University.

Primary sources

Abbreviations

HATa – History of Advertising Trust Archives, Norwich.

JWTa – J. Walter Thompson Archive, Hartman Center, Duke University, North Carolina.

HOYTa – Hoyt Archive, Hartman Center, Duke University, North Carolina.

CBa – Charles Barker Archive, Guildhall Library, London.

AYERa – NW Ayer Archive, National Museum of American History, Smithsonian Institute.

Account files, Boxes 1, JWTa

Agencies Box, HATa

Charles Barker Letters Book 1825–1847 MS 20011, CBa.

Bernstein Company History Files, Biographical File Series, Box 4, JWTa.

Chipchase, Paul (c. 1977) Manuscript notes on Streets, Streets File, HATa.

Colmans file, HATa.

Crowsley, E. G. (c. 1951) 'James White'. Unpublished notes for the Charles Lamb Society, Whites Box HATa.

Darrow, Paul, n.d. *Recollections*, Oral History transcript, AYERa.

Derriman, James, n.d. 'Something in the City: the first 100 years of Charles Barker and Son'. Unpublished manuscript, Agencies Box, HATa.

Hoyt, Charles (1926) Agency Training Manual, HOYTa.

Streets n.d. 'The Story of Streets'. Unpublished manuscript.

Twin Peaks (1996) Exhibition Leaflet. D&AD Festival of Design and Advertising, 27 November – 1 December.

RF White Box; HATa.

CULTURAL STUDIES 16(4) 2002, 553–569

Routledge
Taylor & Francis Group

Lise Skov

HONG KONG FASHION DESIGNERS AS CULTURAL INTERMEDIARIES: OUT OF GLOBAL GARMENT PRODUCTION

Abstract

Based on an ethnographic study of Hong Kong's fashion world, the article maps the working experiences and career trajectories of Hong Kong fashion designers. It traces their individualistic lifestyle to the project-based teaching methods in design schools, and goes on to examine their relative isolation in the organization structure in the export-oriented garment industry. It discusses the ambivalence of fashion design as 'a young profession', indicating both dynamism and creativity, but also a gradual closure of opportunities as designers grow older. Fashion designers experience many conflicts with bosses and businesspeople in the industry, which they understand in terms of conflicts between 'ideas' and 'money'. Drawing on Adorno, this is analysed as a basic conflictuality in the culture industries. However, unlike many of their Western counterparts, Hong Kong designers self consciously embrace the market as a basic social mechanism for the diffusion of their work. Finally, the article follows fashion designers as they set up their own labels and boutiques. It is argued that they represent a new type of entrepreneur that is distinguished from Hong Kong's old entrepreneurs by their rejection of short-term profit orientation and instrumentalism – which have otherwise been considered to be the mainstays in Hong Kong's entrepreneurial ethos. Even so, it is not easy for a small-scale name designer to stay in business in Hong Kong's competitive retail market, and the large-scale export industry shows little interest in supporting Hong Kong designer fashion. The article contributes to an analysis of the

Cultural Studies ISSN 0950-2386 print/ISSN 1466-4348 online © 2002 Taylor & Francis Ltd
http://www.tandf.co.uk/journals
DOI: 10.1080/09502380210139115

ambivalent role of non-Western cultural intermediaries in culture industries, which although they are globalized are still Euro-centric. The global
flows of culture and economy are so disjunctive that while they empower
Hong Kong fashion designers in some ways, they disempower them in
other ways.

Keywords

cultural intermediaries; fashion design; garment industry; globalization;
Hong Kong

THE STORY OF fashion design in Hong Kong cannot be told without reference to the territory's huge garment industry. Since the 1950s, it has been
one of the world's largest garment exporters, and, under the current conditions
of global manufacturing, it continues to be a nodal point for garment sourcing.
Hong Kong fashion design has literally *grown out of* the industry's need to upgrade
its output in order to capture more valuable segments of its export markets.

Over the years, however, Hong Kong has produced but few international
fashion brands. Most garment companies have remained invisible in the global
subcontracting networks where they manufacture garments for international
labels such as Tommy Hilfiger, the Gap and many others. For local fashion designers, the concentration on subcontracting has been frustrating. They feel that their
professional skills qualify them to more than serving as anonymous technicians,
and they would like to take a leading role in developing international fashion
brands. Frustrations at work lead many to change their career after working for
a few years, while others set up their own company and struggle to survive in
Hong Kong's competitive retail market. In other words, fashion designers have
outgrown the export-oriented industry.

In many ways, their proximity to the huge garment industry benefits Hong
Kong fashion designers. It gives them opportunities to take relatively well-paid
jobs, and through their work they have a good knowledge of how the industry
works – both technically and business-wise. Hong Kong's wholesale markets
offer all kinds of specialized materials and fashion information from all parts of
the world. In addition, small-scale entrepreneurs have access to highly specialized manufacturing facilities, ensuring that short runs of sophisticated garments
can be produced speedily and in high quality. In spite of such advantages, designers perceive the local garment industry more as a hindrance than as an aid to
fashion design.

In this article, I present a collective portrait of Hong Kong fashion designers and their relation to the garment industry based upon an ethnographic study
of thirty practitioners conducted in 1993–8. Inevitably, this will focus on the

similarities between these designers, while downplaying variations and differences. My hope is that with these rather bold strokes I can raise some general issues about non-Western cultural intermediaries who form an important, but largely overlooked, segment of those working in global culture industries. In doing so, I take up Angela McRobbie's suggestion that local ethnographies have a crucial knowledge-generating function, and the following discussion is presented in this vein.

Design and development

In order to tease out the ambivalent position of Hong Kong fashion designers we will start by looking back in time to the development in the 1950s of Hong Kong's export-oriented garment industry. Shaped by the Cold War, a distinctive industrial geography developed that connected a poorly paid labour force of Chinese refugees and sojourners with the world's most sophisticated and profitable consumer markets, which at the time were located in the West. However, as local wages rose, and as more third-world countries began exporting garments to the West, Hong Kong's export strategy of price undercutting was difficult to sustain. Around 1960, the USA and Europe set up the quota system for international fibre trade in order to restrict the growth of garment export from developing industries such as that of Hong Kong. By the mid-1960s, therefore, it had become urgent for Hong Kong garment factories to increase the value of their exports. This is where fashion enters the story.

At that time, leading industrialists took a keen interest in design. They organized a series of public lectures on design for the business community, and they set up the first courses in design in Hong Kong's Technical Institutions. In design studies, fashion tends to be perceived as the frivolous little sister to product design – which has directly grown out of modernism and industrialism. It is remarkable, therefore, that in Hong Kong fashion was given priority. When the newly established Trade Development Council organized its first major trade fair in 1967, it decided to focus on the needs of the garment industry (Turner and Ngan, 1995). The reason was the profitability and sheer size of the garment sector that at the time employed almost half of Hong Kong's labour force. The Hong Kong Trade Development Council's garment trade fair – now known as Hong Kong Fashion Week – continues to be one of Hong Kong's largest trade fairs. A major task of the Hong Kong Trade Development Council has been to provide an image for local industries in their export markets. There is a direct line from the 1967 'Festival of Fashion' – designed to provide an image for *all* Hong Kong industries – to trade delegations today – which continue to present an image of Hong Kong through high-profile fashion shows.

To secure the quality and glamour of such shows, the Council has enlisted local fashion designers to produce catwalk shows for trade delegations. Few designers turn down such an opportunity: in part because they are happy to do something 'for Hong Kong', in part because it gives them a chance to command resources that are normally beyond the reach of a small designer label. However, such trade delegations do not facilitate export orders or expose local designers to the international fashion press. They find themselves in an ambivalent position – central for the image which benefits all industries, but marginal within those industries. Over the years, name designers have therefore come to feel that the trade development council has 'used' them.

Their frustration is aggravated by the fact that design has been a keyword in official discourse since the late 1960s. Political figures and leading industrialists have repeatedly stated that Hong Kong needs to develop its design in order to advance. Design historian Matthew Turner (1990) has pointed out that such statements have more often than not been based on the assumption that good design has to be learned from abroad. They have reinforced the need to monitor, and closely follow, Western consumer markets. Thus, the design-as-progress discourse has reinforced the sense of discontinuous development in that the local past is deemed an inadequate basis of future development. As Turner puts it, '[e]ach statement of progress is also a reiteration of Hong Kong's lack of progress' (1990: 133).

Beneath the continuity of the development discourse and the Trade Development Council's promotional strategy, Hong Kong's garment industry has changed immensely since the 1960s. While it originally gained entry to Western markets by manufacturing long runs of standardized items – for example, men's shirts, women's brassieres and children's clothes – it now specializes in short runs produced for all market segments, including chain stores and designer labels. With the increase in industrial flexibility, the organization of labour and technology has inevitably grown more complex. Thus factories that used to work on two or three styles at any one time may now work on three hundred, and they may accept orders down to a few dozen items (Berger and Lester, 1997: 144–8). The emergence in the 1990s of mass customization – the large-scale marketing of designer labels (Smith, 1997) – would hardly have been possible without the global manufacturing networks in which Hong Kong acts as an intermediary between Western brands and third-world factories.

Hong Kong underwent a major industrial transition in the early 1980s when the establishment of Special Economic Zones in Southern China enabled industrialists to set up factories across the border. Many garment companies have only retained a few specialized functions in Hong Kong – typically management, design, quality control or high-tech production processes – while manual work such as assembly and knitting takes place in Hong Kong-owned or managed factories in China or elsewhere (for example, in the Caribbean, Asia, Europe or North America). Since 1980, the development of Hong Kong's garment industry has consisted primarily in the expansion and spatial segregation of manufacturing.

While there are examples of internationally successful Hong Kong labels – for example, Esprit[1] and Episode[2] – the industry on the whole has not been very active in branding and marketing. It is striking, therefore, that the industry today is faced with basically the same problem as it was in the 1960s. The need to strengthen local design thus reappeared as the major conclusion of the authoritative study of Hong Kong's manufacturing industries conducted in 1996–7 by a team of scholars from the MIT (Berger and Lester, 1997). Indeed, the general weakness of fashion design was singled out as a 'major lost opportunity for Hong Kong'.

At the root of the problem, we find the question of Hong Kong's future development. Soon after the 1997 handover to China, Premier Tung Chee-Wah launched a scheme for turning Hong Kong into a 'design centre', thereby reinstating the design-as-progress discourse of the 1960s. It was clear, however, that the design Tung has in mind has to do with to information technology and finance, while the garment industry is increasingly perceived as a remnant of an earlier industrial phase. In accord with the discontinuous notion of development Hong Kong's unsurpassed expertise in managing globally dispersed manufacturing networks is not highly valued at home.

There are alternative visions, however. The above-mentioned MIT study outlines an increased integration of manufacturing and service industries as a development strategy. The authors summarize this in the belief that 'the high-value-added goods of the twenty-first century will be *service-enhanced* products' (Berger and Lester, 1997: xiii). It is hardly surprising that fashion designers should agree. As cultural intermediaries, their job is to add value to garments, and they have the skills required to transform subcontracting companies to designer-led brand-builders. However, as cultural intermediaries they are rarely powerful enough to decide the business strategy of the organization for which they work, as we will see in the following pages.

Fashion design as profession and identity

Soon after his graduation in 1998, a young fashion designer told me the following: 'It is all a learning process. I am a young designer. This is a young profession. Hong Kong has only just reached the level of an advanced industrialized society. We still have a lot to learn'. I quote this statement here to illustrate the potential homology between individual and socio-economic development. Fashion designers can use the design-as-progress discourse to coalesce their personal trajectory with that of society as a whole – and in the process they make an argument for the growth potential of the fashion business. At the same time, the notion of youth is ambivalent. Bourdieu has analysed social youth as the potential to invest oneself and accumulate capital in a chosen field (Bourdieu, 1984). In this case, however, social youth may also connote continued marginality, especially when we keep in mind that the rhetoric of Hong Kong as an up-and-coming fashion and design centre has been in circulation for more than thirty years.

In Bourdieu's own discussion of cultural intermediaries, he singles out fashion design as a profession that combines high cultural capital with low educational capital. Fashion designers are seen to be the sons and daughters of the old bourgeoisie who make a living out of their natural good manners and taste when – it is hinted – they do not have the intelligence or discipline to succeed in more conventional fields. It is hardly a coincidence that this type of fashion designer is represented, by Bourdieu, in the 'old' fashioned centre of Paris. By contrast, Angela McRobbie has shown that contemporary British fashion designers do not in general come from privileged families; neither are they uneducated (McRobbie, 1998). The same point is valid for Hong Kong fashion designers. There *are* examples of socialite designers among Hong Kong's 'big names', although, in colonial society, the problem of protecting old class privileges from social erosion is complicated by the ambivalent status of the local elites.

More important is the fact that, with a sustained growth rate of over ten per cent per year, Hong Kong society *as a whole* has been upwardly mobile since the 1960s. The education sector has expanded considerably so that sons and daughters of working-class parents often receive secondary and tertiary education today. High growth rates have also secured a dramatic rise in family incomes, in turn lending credibility to the widespread myth that Hong Kong offers fair rewards for all who are prepared to work hard (Lui and Wong, 1994).

Scholars studying Hong Kong families have tended to view them as economic units controlling the incomes and careers prospects of its members by strategically pooling together its resources. The best known example is Janet Salaff's study, _conducted in the 1970s, of elder daughters who were taken out of school at an early age to work in the factories in order to pay for the education of their younger siblings (Salaff, 1981/1995). While economic growth and industrial transition has outdated this practice, scholars continue to note a tendency for Chinese parents to have a strong say with regard to the education and careers of their children (Greenhalgh, 1994; Ong, 1998). It is therefore remarkable that although many of the designers I have interviewed have been supported by their parents to go through tertiary education, none has been encouraged to take up fashion.

We may not be surprised to learn that upper-class parents are worried when their elder sons want to study fashion. For example, William Tang – a member of one of the land-owning lineages in the New Territories and probably Hong Kong's best known designer – was required to do a degree in economics before he was allowed to enter a London art school to study fashion. Similarly, Barney Cheng – of urban upper-class background and the most successful Hong Kong designer in the late 1990s – reached a compromise with his father that he would study architecture (which was seen to combine his aesthetic sensibility with some respectability) while in fact, he ended up graduating in fine arts. However, these designers are exceptions.

For our purpose, it is more interesting that many working-class and middle-class parents do not see fashion as a secure field. Fashion students told me that their parents would rather see them study medicine or computer science. Worries about future income weigh heavily (but not exclusively) on male students, in contrast to the mid-1980s when many tailors sent their sons to design school so that they could pass their trade on to the next generation. Apart from indicating the general symbolic devaluation of fashion design in Hong Kong, this change also shows that fashion design is an increasingly individualistic profession. In fact, many students and young designers have a strong emotional involvement with fashion which is incomprehensible to their parents. The individualism of fashion design is strengthened in the design schools where they are forced to rely on their *own* ideas and experiences through project work, which is otherwise uncommon in Hong Kong's education system. In school, 'critical judgement' is perceived to be a bulwark against mindless reproduction of trends, while in the work place, designers need a good dose of self confidence to stand up for their ideas among business people.

Bourdieu has pointed out that the work of cultural intermediaries tends to be related to the body. This is certainly true of fashion design. Not only do fashion designers dress other bodies, they learn to use their own bodies as aesthetic measures. Thus, fashion designers talk about having 'a good eye' – the sense of aesthetic judgement – and having 'good hands' – the ability to work with the fabric during fittings. In addition, designers learn to talk about their work in specific ways. The fact that they speak eloquently about their likes and dislikes make them stand out in Hong Kong where schools tend not to encourage self expression and where young people usually keep quiet in front of their seniors (cf. Lilley, 1998: 139). Fashion education thus involves 'the whole person' to the extent that it is impossible to draw a line between professional creative skills and self expression.

At the same time, the requirements of the profession give the designer self a standardized form, exemplified in the *portfolio* that all fashion students compile. Every young fashion designer I have talked to told me that their future dream is to create their own label. In fact, they find this ambition so evident that they are hardly able to explain it. 'It is just like an artist wants to create an art work', one designer said in response to my prodding. As we will see in the following, many young Hong Kong designers do in fact have the opportunity to launch their own label – though hardly under the conditions they had hoped for.

Fashion designers and the garment industry

The garment industry is the biggest employer of fashion designers in Hong Kong. Here, they make clothes for any conceivable market segment in practically all parts of the world. Some work for local chain stores such as G2000, Giordano or Reno and Donna. Others are employed by export companies where they make collections, for example, for mail order firms or department store in-house labels. Given the industry's strength in casualwear and knitwear, many designers specialize in these fields. By the late 1990s, the industry's traditional reliance on exports to the West gave way to a focus on Asian markets. Thus many designers work for Japanese companies or with Japanese partners, and many Hong Kong chain stores have outlets in other countries in the region. Towards the end of the decade, the consumer market in China grew considerably, providing jobs for an increasing number of Hong Kong designers.

When fashion designers told me about their work in the industry, their stories were full of frustrations. A senior designer, who was working with fashion promotion at the time of the interview, summarized the experiences of many designers in the following way:

> I was lucky because in my company it was always the boss that made the final decisions. If he liked my work it was OK. But in other companies there are too many people who make decisions. Maybe the designer has to change something because the buyer doesn't like it, and then it has to be changed again because the senior merchandiser doesn't like it. I even know of a place where the pattern maker sends everything back to the designer unless it is done very precisely. So you have to do a lot to keep up a good relationship with the pattern maker. That is why they call it a *people industry*. You have to get on with people to get by. You need a pleasant personality. I have heard many designers complain that they are not treated professionally.

Whether employed on a full-time or a freelance basis, fashion designers tend to occupy a marginal position in the organizational structure. Many are employed as the only designer in a company. Others have designer colleagues, but working on separate projects. Some companies even foster rivalry among junior designers by making them compete for the favours of the boss. Thus, all the young designers in my sample have had the experience of presenting and defending their work alone without the support of a senior designer or a design team.

Designers often complain that their employers do not understand that fashion design is different from other work in the garment business. For example, they would like to work in spacious and aesthetically appealing studios, and when there is no immediate work in the office they would like to take time off to go window shopping or visit a gallery. Instead they have to clock in and out every day. Their work spaces are cramped and often without windows. Some designers even work next to the sewing machine operators.

Like the majority of Hong Kong residents, fashion designers work long hours, often until nine or ten in the evening. They change jobs often, sometimes every few months. Interpersonal conflicts is a major reason, as is the opportunity to claim a higher salary in a different company. In addition, many change jobs in order to develop their professional skills by working with different types of clothing or in different types of organizations.

A common observation among businesspeople is that designers 'run dry' after a few seasons. Designers may not disagree. In fact, many complain of being exhausted, and of feeling less creative the longer they work. However, whereas the company bosses draw the conclusion that investment in fashion designers should be kept to a minimum – by only employing freelance designers for specific orders, for example – designers argue that their problems are caused by the industry investing to *too little* in fashion. In fact, the position of fashion design in Hong Kong's garment industry conforms to economic sociologist Paul Hirsch's model of the culture industry system in which creative work is marginalized in the organizational structure. In this system, 'contracted artists [. . .] are *delegated* the responsibility of producing marketable creations, with little or no inter-ference from the front office beyond the setting of budgetary limits'. Hirsch argues that this system has been developed in response to the 'widespread uncer-tainty over the precise ingredients of a best-seller formula' (Hirsch, 1972/1992: 367).

The organizational isolation of fashion design is in many ways a continuation of the industry's reliance on overseas buyers' specifications. This has typically worked in the way that designers in, say, New York or Dusseldorf have faxed a drawing or a production sketch to the Hong Kong company where it has been 'translated' into a sample. This has required a high degree of standardization of work processes. We should not forget, either, that through most of the post-war period, local tastes have been at odds with Western consumer trends, and differ-ences have inevitably been interpreted as a sign of Hong Kong's backwardness. As we have seen, the benevolent interpretation of this has been that 'Hong Kong needs to learn from the West'. As a contrast to this routine, senior fashion design-ers told me of their hopes for collaboration between professional groups centred around a design concept, combining the region's cheap labour and technological expertise with design visions. Ultimately, this would replace the technical orien-tation of the engineers who have dominated the garment industry with the creative orientation of fashion designers. In reality, however, the number of large designer-led fashion brands in Hong Kong can be counted on the fingers of one hand.

While many fashion designers lament the absence of such companies, their actual experiences and ambitions indicate a more complex situation. Young designers treasure their independence and high income – which they enjoy exactly because of the reification of fashion design as a 'young profession'. In 1997, the salary of a fresh graduate was HK$10–14,000 (which is high compared to Europe). After five to eight years, they reach a maximum around HK$35,000. Compared to the income pattern of fashion merchandisers, designers have a high starting salary, but they have relatively few opportunities to advance their career after five to ten years of work.

Is this then an exploitation of a young and enthusiastic workforce? Indeed, fashion designers are responsible employees because they invest themselves in their work, at the same time as their youth, and to some extent their gender, block them from being powerful within the organization. It is not hard to find examples of freelance designers being paid less than the promised fee, or full-timers may be laid off in irregular ways in order to preclude them from insisting on their labour rights. However, we should not forget that fashion designers are not worse off than other employees in Hong Kong's companies that have long been renowned for evading labour rights (England, 1989; Woodiwiss, 1998). However, the biggest problem with the notion of exploitation is that it reduces the personal investment in creative work by viewing it through the lens of instrumentalism.

Ideas versus money

When fashion designers told me about their work they singled out a scenario that more than anything else represented their conflicts and frustrations. This scenario centred upon the negotiations between designers and business people that take place when designers presented a collection. Item by item they go over the collection with buyers or merchandisers to discuss style, cost and production in order to make the necessary changes. In the course of the production of a collection this scenario is repeated a couple of times.

An example comes from a 25-year-old woman designer, working for a Hong Kong chain store. One season, she had made the sketches and production drawings for a blouse with mandarin collar and string buttons. On the whole, young Hong Kong women – the target consumers of the chain store – wear culturally neutral styles. However, the designer was curious about using Chinese elements in her design, and she was convinced that such a blouse could sell if only it was made in an unexpected fabric, such as denim, 'so that it wouldn't look *too* Chinese'. When she presented this blouse to the company buyers, their first comment was that 'Hong Kong Chinese don't want to buy Oriental styles'. When she explained that she wanted to make it in denim to make in unusual, the buyers turned to last year's sale figures, and said that 'denim doesn't sell well, either'. So it was out of the question to produce the blouse. Reflecting on her experience, she said that 'buyers are very keen on figures, but they are not good at analyzing *the reason why*'. When she and other designers talk about such experiences, they outline a confrontation between 'ideas' and 'money'. On the one hand we have designers with a holistic way of thinking, which allows for a certain degree of aesthetic autonomy. On the other hand, we have the business people who analytically split up the elements of the idea. The problem – designer stress – is not the need to compromise, but the fact that a compromise is reached on unequal terms. Many conflicts break out over deadlines. If a designer is not satisfied with a style, she might ask to have another sample made to supervise the final changes. Even if this can be done in a single day, it can still mean a considerable loss in terms of unused factory capacity. Add to this the fact that designers pride themselves of being good at details (this brings to mind Roland Barthes's definition of fashion as shifting *accents* (1967/1983)). They have a professional interest in the shape of a lapel or the nuance and texture of a fabric – which they rarely share with garment merchandisers. One designer characterized the business people in her company in the following way: 'If we agree we are going to do an item in orange, they are not the sort of people who will sit down and discuss whether the nuance should be paprika or chilli'. By contrast, designers might well find such a discussion worthwhile. The point here is that a detail, for which a designer is prepared to delay production, may seem marginal, or simply impractical, to the businesspeople responsible for the production process.

How can we understand their experience of the conflict between ideas and money? Here it is important to remember that Hong Kong designers do not lament the commercial nature of fashion. They are not against the market, and they do not believe that creativity is enhanced by a disavowal of business interests. In this respect, they differ not only from artists, but also from the young British fashion designers who use a variety of discursive strategies to distance themselves from the commercial nature of fashion (McRobbie, 1998). By contrast, Hong Kong fashion designers are fascinated by the way the market works, and they perceive it as a basic *social* mechanism for the diffusion of fashion. When I have prodded into the limits of commercialism, the figure that to their minds embodies the bracketing off of the economy is not the heroic artist – in many ways a Western construction – but the pigheaded garment boss who overrules the designer's ideas with his own quirky taste. So how can we understand this insistence on ideas within the commercial realm? Here I wish to bring in Theodor W. Adorno's work on the culture industry (1991; with M. Horkheimer, 1997). He is usually read as a severe and purist critic of the culture industry. However, I find his work useful because it is saturated with an ambivalence that echoes the conflicts between ideas and money that are played out in the Hong Kong fashion business.

For Adorno, the culture industry is defined as a struggle between art and cultural commodities. The art work embodies autonomy – in the sense of reliance on internal logic and freedom from economic interests 'which of course rarely ever predominated in an entirely pure form'. In cultural commodities this autonomy is thoroughly debased because '[c]ultural commodities typical of the culture industry are no longer *also* commodities, they are commodities through and through' (Adorno, 1991: 86). In my reading, the essential point is that the utopian element in art – which Adorno identifies as never-fully-realized – is never completely irretrievable, either. Hong Kong fashion designers retrieve it by insisting on some degree of creative autonomy.

In using Adorno in this way it should be clear that I do not subscribe to the standard criticism of him for being elitist (not because this is entirely wrong, but because it is essentially a toothless criticism). As I see it, the problem with Adorno is that he is speaking from a purely philosophical bird's eye perspective in which social life is lost of sight. He does not have much to offer on the ways in which the production of art and culture are embedded in social structures. However, his work is valuable in pointing to a basic conflictuality between 'culture' and 'industry' or in the words of Hong Kong fashion designers 'ideas' and 'money'. What Adorno calls the two-faced irony of the culture industry is acted out as an everyday drama in the global fashion business with designers and business people holding opposing roles. We might say that there is a good deal of naivety in Adorno's insistence on the autonomy of art, despite his qualifications. Yet it is exactly this naivety – this insistence on the autonomy of the aesthetic enterprise in the face of overpowering economic calculation – that Hong Kong's fashion designers share with Adorno.

Reluctant entrepreneurs

Some years after graduation, fashion designers begin to find that they have few opportunities to advance their career. Many feel exhausted from ongoing conflicts, and even bored with the seasonal rhythm of fashion. At this stage, many change their careers, for example, by moving into marketing or merchandising, either in fashion or related fields. Some seek work as fashion teachers in the design schools or as administrators in the Trade Development Council's fashion office. Others set up their own companies. In this section, I will concentrate on the last group, which make up Hong Kong's 'name' designers.

I have already mentioned that practically all fashion designers share the dream of creating their own label. By becoming self-employed they have the opportunity to realize this dream, and it may therefore seem to be a logical career move. However, they leave the industry with mixed feelings. They face the problem of managing a small company that may be involved in everything from manufacturing to export and retail. They look in vain for consultancy about management and marketing. Also, they have to replace the global reach of a large Hong Kong company for a local operation, entering a saturated retail market where they have to complete with international brand name stores clustered in elegant shopping centres where real estate prices are high.

In spite of these obstacles, it has been quite common among young designers to try their luck as entrepreneurs. Many have set up a small boutique in the Beverly Centre in Tsim Sha Tsui or in nearby Rise Commercial Building. The retail space here is only a small cubicle, but even so rent claims one third of the garments' retail price. Some of Hong Kong's established designers – such as Pacino Wan, Ruby Li and Benjamin Lau – have had their boutiques here for years, while many others go bust within the first year of operation. They follow a trajectory 'from getting started to going bust' – spanning from an initial enthusiasm to permanent cash flow problems and exhaustion when eventually the company is closed down – similar to the trajectory which McRobbie found in her study of British designers (1998). However, there are important differences.

Firstly, in contrast to their British counterparts, Hong Kong fashion entrepreneurs do not receive any government benefits. They pool the necessary investments together from savings and loans, typically from their parents. In addition, they often freelance for the industry to make ends meet – and, of course, they have good opportunities to take such jobs. Hence they are more steeped in market relations than British fashion designers.

A second difference from the UK is that the fragmented nature of Hong Kong's garment industry provides a stimulating environment for fashion entrepreneurs. They can shop around highly specialized wholesale markets to compare fabrics and accessories imported from all parts of the world, and buy small amounts at cheap prices. For made-to-measure orders they can employ a highly skilled seamstress for a day rate of HK$200.

By contrast, McRobbie describes manufacturing as the difficult part of British fashion design. It is often done by family and friends or by the designers themselves. McRobbie also describes some degree of ignorance of manufacturing processes – for example, when designers unable to calculate fabric consumption are cheated by their contractors. I have not found this to be a problem in Hong Kong where fashion designers are much more familiar with the production process.

Having made a point for the dominance of market relations in Hong Kong, it must be added that fashion designers are at the same time the beneficiaries of public funds through the Trade Development Council. In contrast to what we might expect from the official *laissez-faire* rhetoric, the Hong Kong government supports local fashion at a level unsurpassed anywhere in the world. However, as I have discussed earlier, this is part of its strategy to provide an image for all Hong Kong industries, and specific concerns of fashion designers come second to this.

Ultimately, the biggest difference between Hong Kong and British fashion designers is the overall cultural and economic environment in which they work. McRobbie traces the mixed roots of recent British fashion to subcultural styles, the art school environment with its insistence on the high cultural nature of fashion, the 1980s and 1990s market deregulation. In McRobbie's argument for a revaluation of the process of *making*, we also hear an echo of the British craft tradition. In the beginning of this article, I discussed the developmentalism that provides a somewhat ambivalent context for Hong Kong fashion design. The fact that Hong Kong is a producer society (though not exclusively so) has rather mixed effects on the fashion business. On the one hand, I have described how fashion designers are treated as outsiders, even slightly suspicious figures, in an environment where others work for money. On the other hand, the business-oriented environment offers them the means to realize their fashion ambitions.

Scholars talk about a Hong Kong ethos on the basis of three elements: the entrepreneurial spirit, desire for social mobility and profit-orientation, which are clearly linked to the experience of exile and to the territory's rapid economic growth (Lau and Kuan, 1988; Lui and Wong, 1994). Compared to this, fashion designers represent a new type of entrepreneur for whom the company is not primarily a means to make money and advance socially. In fact, designers tend to see short-term profit-orientation as detrimental to the development of a label. One designer-entrepreneur presented the following reflections:

> Some of my friends advise me on how to make money quickly. But I don't want to rush things. It is easy to survive if you know what you want. People in Hong Kong are lucky; they can eat; they can find a place to live; it is easy to get a job. My dream is not to make a lot of money. All I want is a happy lifestyle. Designers only get frustrated if they see fashion as a way of making money. My principle is work hard and don't expect too much.

As this designer indicates, many experience the tendency to measure success in money as a pressure that they must defuse. They do so by pointing to the overall wealth of Hong Kong, and by redefining entrepreneurship from an instrumental activity to a lifestyle. Even so, many name designers experience frustrations because even when they are quite successful, it is practically impossible to consolidate a small designer label without financial backing. This problem points us back to the large garment manufacturers. They have the size and the global networks to support small fashion labels, but name designers have looked in vain for the sustained backing it would take for a Hong Kong designer to make an impact in, for example, Paris or New York.

Fashion designers represent a new type of entrepreneur in Hong Kong. They replace the instrumental attitude of the old entrepreneurs with something which – borrowing a phrase from Paul du Gay (1997) – we may call the cultural economy to indicate an increasing integration of culture and economy. They eclectically embrace elements of the Hong Kong ethos, especially the value of hard work, while discarding others such as the short-term profit-orientation and the instrumentalism. In this way, their entrepreneurship can be seen as a critical practice against the Hong Kong's entrepreneurs who built the export-oriented garment industry. As we can expect from cultural intermediaries, however, it is a criticism that fully embraces the conditions of global capitalism as it tries to change them.

Conclusion: mediating the local and the global

Hong Kong fashion designers are mediators between production and consumption. At the same time, they are also cultural intermediaries in the sense of mediating between East and West, between the global and the local.

They are not the first people in Hong Kong to do this. In fact, the old entrepreneurs were mediators between the local labour force and Western consumer markets. In this globalization *avant la lettre*, the meeting between East and West was regulated by a dualistic cultural model that can be traced back to the nineteenth century. While a nationalist slogan such as 'Chinese learning for the foundation, Western learning for application' seems outdated, this kind of dualism nevertheless still represents a local model for 'striking a bargain' between modernity and difference, as Ulf Hannerz puts it (1996: 55). The dualism of Western materialism/Chinese spirit reappears also in much recent scholarship with its search for Chineseness in the intangible (so-called cultural) aspects of a highly Westernized economy.

The problem of Hong Kong fashion designers is that they do not fit into this dualistic cultural model. In fact, their work upsets any clearcut distinction between Western technology and Chinese spirit. Throughout this article we have seen examples of this. The fact that fashion design involves the 'whole person' perches designers across the divide between 'Chinese knowledge for foundation' and 'Western knowledge for application'. Their personal investment in their work counters the instrumental orientation of the industry. Their individualism and skills in self presentation upset organizational hierarchies based on age and gender in a way that is popularly interpreted as 'Western' individualism vs. 'Chinese' authoritarianism. As cultural intermediaries, Hong Kong fashion designers represent a different kind of cultural blending – one which dissolves the polarities between East and West and between culture and economy. This is seen most clearly, perhaps, in the curiousity many designers have in using Chinese aesthetics in their design. This can be done in many different ways. Earlier we saw an example of a designer wanting to make a standard Chinese blouse in an unusual fabric. This was thought out for a chain store, and more sophisticated name designers may look down on such an attempt to use 'Chinese elements'. However, when they apply Chinese concepts in such a way that their designs question the unity of both Chinese and Western elements, they are actually involved in a similar project. Both transform Hong Kong's cultural dualism of Chinese tradition and Western modernity from a regulated cultural sterility to a fertile meeting ground from which something new can emerge.

Notes

1   Hong Kong Esprit is marketed worldwide except for the USA. Due to a complicated company history, Esprit US and Esprit Hong Kong share the same logo but are otherwise completely unrelated companies.
2   Episode is the main label of Toppy, a retail company of the Fang Brothers Knitting Factory. Additional labels are Jessica, Jeselle, Excursion and Colour Eighteen.

References

Adorno, Theodor W. (1991) *The Culture Industry*. Edited by J. M. Bernstein. London: Routledge.

Adorno, Theodor W. and Horkheimer, Max (1944/1997) *Dialectic of Enlightenment*. London: Verso.

Barthes, Roland (1967/1983) *The Fashion System*. Berkeley, CA: University of California Press.

Berger, Barbara and Lester, Richard K. (eds) (1997) *Made By Hong Kong*. Hong Kong: Oxford University Press.

Bourdieu, Pierre (1984) *Distinction: A Social Critique of the Judgement of Taste*. London: Routledge and Kegan Paul.

Du Gay, Paul (ed.) (1997) *Production of Culture/Culture of Production*. London: Sage, with Open University.

England, Joe (1989) *Industrial Relations and Law in Hong Kong*, 2nd edn. Hong Kong: Oxford University Press.

Featherstone, Mike (1991) *Consumer Culture and Postmodernism*. London: Sage.

Greenhalgh, Susan (1994) 'De-orientalizing the Chinese family firm'. *American Ethnologist*, 21(4): 746–76.

Hannerz, Ulf (1996) *Transnational Connections: Culture, People, Places*. London: Routledge.

Hirsch, Paul (1972/1992) 'Processing fads and fashions: an organization-set analysis of cultural industry systems'. In M. Granovetter and R. Swedberg (eds) *The Sociology of Economic Life*. Boulder: Westview Press, 363–84.

Lilley, Rozanna (1998) *Staging Hong Kong: Gender and Performance in Transition*. London: Curzon.

Lau, Siu-Kai and Kuan, Hsin-Chi (1988) *The Ethos of the Hong Kong Chinese*. Hong Kong: Chinese University Press.

Lui, Tai Lok and Wong, Thomas (1994) *Chinese Entrepreneurs in Context*. Hong Kong: The Hong Kong Institute of Asia Pacific Studies.

McRobbie, Angela (1998) *British Fashion Design: Rag Trade or Image Industry?* London: Routledge.

Ong, Aihwa (1998) 'Flexible citizenship among Chinese cosmopolitans'. In Ph. Cheah and B. Robbins (eds) *Cosmopolitics: Thinking and Feeling beyond the Nation*. Minneapolis: Minnesota University Press, 134–63.

Salaff, Janet W. (1981/1995) *Working Daughters of Hong Kong: Filial Piety or Power in the Family?* New York: Columbia University Press.

Smith, Paul (1997) 'Tommy Hilfiger in the age of mass customization'. In Andrew Ross (ed.) *No Sweat: Fashion, Free Trade and the Rights of Garment Workers.* New York: Verso, 249–263.

Turner, Matthew (1990) 'Development and transformation in the discourse of design in Hong Kong'. In Rajeshwari Ghose (ed.) *Design and Development in South and Southeast Asia.* Hong Kong: Centre for Asian Studies, University of Hong Kong, 123–37.

Turner, Matthew and Ngan, Irene (eds) (1995) *Hong Kong Sixties: Designing Identity.* Hong Kong: Hong Kong Arts Centre.

Woodiwiss, Anthony (1998) *Globalisation, Human Rights and Labour Law in Pacific Asia.* Cambridge: Cambridge University Press.

CULTURAL STUDIES 16(4) 2002, 570–592

Routledge
Taylor & Francis Group

Matthew Soar

THE FIRST THINGS FIRST MANIFESTO AND THE POLITICS OF CULTURE JAMMING: TOWARDS A CULTURAL ECONOMY OF GRAPHIC DESIGN AND ADVERTISING

Abstract

Advertising has long been recognized as an important cultural force by media and cultural studies scholars. Graphic design, despite its comparable ubiquity, has rarely been the subject of this kind of critique. Where these activities *have* been discussed, the emphasis has been overwhelmingly on their textual manifestations (graphics, ads, commercials) and, occasionally, on their reception. In the interest of working towards a fuller account of the overall circulation and reproduction of an increasingly commercial contemporary culture, then, this paper turns to the generative source of these ephemeral artefacts and, in particular, professional graphic design practice. By paying especial attention to the framing of current debates about accountability and social responsibility *within* this profession, this paper seeks to explore the constraining and enabling effects of commercial practice. Advertising and design are readily distinguishable from other economic institutions because of their declared expertise in creating specifically *cultural* forms of communication. Further, these practices rely on the skills of cultural intermediaries: individuals whose job it is to develop these forms to mediate between, or more properly, *articulate*, the realms of production and consumption. Graphic designers, it seems, enjoy much greater latitude for personal expression than ad creatives – or at least enjoy a professional culture, or habitus, that supports debate and dissent through a variety of activities, and recognizes non-commercial design

Cultural Studies ISSN 0950-2386 print/ISSN 1466-4348 online © 2002 Taylor & Francis Ltd
http://www.tandf.co.uk/journals
DOI: 10.1080/09502380210139124

projects as legitimate forms of expression. While the designers inter-viewed here may claim that advertising is a creative practice entirely subsumed by commercial constraints, they also recognize that their own professional activities involve only a limited degree of subjective control. Personal and non-commercial projects, often indirectly funded by income from business clients, appear to provide a more reliable means to creative fulfillment.

Keywords

graphic design; advertising; cultural intermediaries; ethics; cultural pro-duction; cultural economy

THIS ARTICLE CONCERNS the contemporary culture of graphic design[1] practice in the USA and, to a lesser degree, that of its close relative, adver-tising. The work presented here is part of a larger project conceived as a response to both the general absence of critical approaches to the study of graphic design and to the dominance of textual approaches to the critical study of advertising (Soar, 2000). It is also part of a project to broaden our limited understanding of a group of workers Pierre Bourdieu (1984) has identified as the 'cultural inter-mediaries'.[2]

Graphic designers and advertising creatives (art directors and copywriters) fit squarely within this last category. Indeed, their working lives depend for their efficacy and ultimate success on a specific attunement to the swirl of values and tastes within culture. More than that, they play an important role in lending traction to the contemporary routines of capital accumulation by articulating these values and tastes to the promotion of ideas and events, services and products. The privileged position the intermediaries hold in the 'circuit of culture' (Johnson, 1986/87) has recently been expressed through the notion of an attenuated, or 'short', circuit (Soar, 2000). How then to bring a critical cultural analysis to bear on these commercial practices? In essence, I am inter-ested in applying a modified cultural studies perspective to these forms of com-mercial practice.[3] In doing so, I align myself with recent scholarship in 'cultural economy' (du Gay, 1996, 1997; du Gay et al., 1997; Nixon, 1997a, b; McRobbie, 1998, 2000) to address the reported investments of the design and advertising intermediaries in the cultural work that they perform. I focus on their values and opinions and highlight the relative sense of empowerment they claim for them-selves. At the heart of this analysis is a short, polemical document called the 'First Things First Manifesto', which calls, in part, for a 'reversal of priorities in favor of more useful, lasting and democratic forms of communication – a mindshift away from product marketing'. It continues: 'Consumerism is running uncontested; it must be challenged by other perspectives expressed, in part, through the visual languages and resource of design'.

Concurrently, the last decade has seen an escalation in the promotion of 'culture jamming' as a viable form of populist, anti-commercial critique. For many people this is most closely associated with the insistent editorial stance of the Canadian magazine *Adbusters*, perhaps best known for its spoof ads deriding a whole range of ills associated with excessive consumerism and the corporate concentration of media ownership, and the promotion of activities such as Buy Nothing Day and TV TurnOff Week. It was also intimately involved with the re-emergence of First Things First.

These two moments – the manifesto proper and *Adbusters'* framing of both First Things First *and* culture jamming – are investigated here because they are directly addressed at the intermediaries *by* intermediaries. Most significantly, they identify designers in particular as potent agents of positive social change.[4] Indeed, if it were not for interventions such as these, in which cultural intermediaries themselves have challenged the priorities of the commercial fields in which they work, then these professions and their associated activities might be far less worthy of our critical attention than their textual manifestations (as currently seems to be the case).

The return of the First Things First manifesto

> When power and control are foremost, moral purpose is reduced to whatever is popular in the marketplace of ideas and commerce, rather than to what is right. This is the guiding principle of bad marketing and bad advertising, and it is also the guiding principle of bad design.
>
> (Buchanan, 1998: 7)

The First Things First manifesto is a call for social responsibility that was signed by and distributed amongst designers, art directors and writers on design through six key periodicals in 1999. It was originally conceived in 1964 as a provisional response to a new social climate characterized by 'the high-pitched scream of consumer selling'. British designer Ken Garland wrote the first draft during a meeting of the Society of Industrial Artists in London in 1963. The manifesto was then signed by twenty-two individuals, many of them well-known photographers, typographers, designers and teachers. It received exposure in, for example, *Modern Publicity*, *Design* and the *Guardian*. Garland was also interviewed on television (see Poynor, 1999, for a concise history).

Interest in the manifesto was rekindled when it was republished in its original form in the mid-nineties in *Eye: The International Review of Graphic Design*, *Emigre [sic]* and *Adbusters: The Journal of the Mental Environment* (published in England, the USA and Canada, respectively). *Eye* republished it in support of an article by Andrew Howard called 'There is such a thing as society' (Howard, 1994), in which he envisioned a post-Thatcherite future of 'partnerships and collaborations in which design is not simply a means to sell and persuade' (Howard, 1994: 77). *Adbusters* republished the original manifesto because its art director, Chris Dixon, and its editor and copublisher, Kalle Lasn, had seen it in *Eye*. Subsequently, several individuals got together to update it, including Lasn, Dixon and Rick Poynor, a distinguished writer on design issues and visual communication (and, until recently, a visiting lecturer at the Royal College of Art in London).

In the autumn of 1999, the newly drafted manifesto ('First Things First 2000') appeared in at least six journals, including *Emigre, AIGA Journal of Graphic Design*[5] and *Adbusters* in North America, *Eye* and *Blueprint* in the UK, and, on the European Continent, *Items* (and, much later, *Form*). It carried Ken Garland's name once more, augmented by those of thirty-two new signatories. In his short article on the history of First Things First, Poynor (1999) stated: 'The vast majority of design projects – and certainly the most lavishly funded and widely disseminated – address corporate needs, a massive over-emphasis on the commercial sector of society, which consumes most of graphic designers' time, skills and creativity' (1999: 56). He thereby made a vital distinction between this singular, commercial role of graphic design and 'the possibility . . . that design might have broader purposes, potential and meanings'. Katherine McCoy, an American design educator, had earlier expressed the situation thus:

> Designers must break out of the obedient, neutral, servant-to-industry mentality, an orientation that was particularly strong in the Reagan/Thatcher 1980s. . . . Design is not a neutral, value-free process. A design has no more integrity than its purpose or subject matter.
>
> (McCoy, 1994: 111)

The manifesto could not fail to make waves when it was republished precisely because it stands in stark contrast to the stock-in-trade of many design magazines. Indeed, part of its critique concerns the intermediaries' apparent obsession with aesthetics and personalities (i.e. design and designers, art and art directors, illustration and illustrators, photography and photographers) – at least as it is endlessly expressed in the majority of design and advertising publications. Eminent among these are so-called 'showcase' or 'portfolio' magazines such as *Communication Arts* (also known as *CA*), *Print, Graphis* and *ID*,[6] all of which are high-gloss productions that use sumptuous photography and printing techniques to show off the latest graphic, packaging, furniture, interior and industrial design (and, less often, their creators). As American designer and critic Michael Rock has noted, 'we have a lot of information about logos and typefaces and the design "heroes" that make them, but little that situates the work in the culture. We need both types of analysis' (Poynor and Rock, 1995: 58).

The chief exceptions to this generally laudatory editorial pattern are *Eye*, the *AIGA Journal of Graphic Design*,[7] *Critique*,[8] and *Emigre*.[9] While they are all just as meticulously crafted in their appearance, these periodicals generally sustain a more reflective or critical editorial stance than their glitzy counterparts. Instead of merely showcasing, they often advance well-researched visual and textual essays that grapple with the social, cultural, historical and political dimensions of design and advertising.[10]

While it has often been said that 'designers don't read', it is clear that some designers at least *write*. Indeed, even a casual familiarity with the design press reveals that there is a core constituency of designer/writers who have produced, collectively, a substantial – if eclectic – body of insightful writing about the dynamics of the profession and its place in culture (see, for example, the articles and essays collected in Bierut *et al.*, 1994, 1997; Heller and Finamore, 1997).[11] These writers are often successful and even distinguished practitioners who have turned to writing perhaps as a way to elaborate ideas that cannot be addressed in depth through the act of designing itself.

As the profession grows in size and visibility, the available avenues for publishing articles and essays have also expanded (as have the number of opportunities to discuss, debate, and present research on design matters).[12] One recent estimate, in a new journal called simply *[. . .]* (i.e. 'dot-dot-dot') showed that the number of graphic design and visual culture magazines in the Northern hemisphere has increased exponentially from around 26 in the early 1950s to over 144 in 2000. The USA currently has 44, while the UK and Germany are able to sustain 52 each (*[. . .]*, 2000: 53). It is perhaps unsurprising, then, that the list of signatories of the relaunched manifesto was largely made up of designer/writers already familiar to many members of the profession.

The following section reports on a series of personal interviews[13] with prominent individuals[14] carried out in late 1999, some of whom put their names to First Things First 2000. The most important theme that has so far emerged from this ongoing field research is the issue of personal and political agency, including some remarkably candid observations on the ways in which this is constrained.

The usual suspects

Michael Bierut is a partner at Pentagram, an international design company of considerable standing among design professionals, and, at the time of interviewing, was president of the AIGA. He has also co-edited a number of works that rightly belong in the category of design criticism (Bierut *et al.*, 1994, 1997, 1999; Kalman *et al.*, 1998). Stefan Sagmeister has a small design company in New York and has produced CD covers for artists such as The Rolling Stones and Lou Reed (see Hall and Sagmeister, 2001). He has been featured in various design magazines for his innovative and occasionally shocking work, and is a popular speaker at art schools and conferences. His favourite personal aphorism is 'style equals fart'. Jessica Helfand runs her own design partnership in Connecticut with William Drenttel, also a designer and past-president of the AIGA. They have only recently moved out of New York City. Helfand has taught at Yale for six years, and has been a writer for *Eye* magazine for four years. She was among the co-editors of *Looking Closer 3: Classic Writings on Graphic Design* (Bierut *et al.*, 1999) and has written two essays on Paul Rand (Helfand, 1998), one among a small group of (male) designers consistently identified as seminal figures in the history of US graphic design. (During his lifetime, Rand also taught students – including Helfand – at Yale.) Milton Glaser is another key figure comparable to Rand; he is exceedingly well-known as a designer, illustrator and educator (see, for example, Glaser, 2000). Glaser[15] has taught for many years at the School of Visual Arts in New York and was a partner in Pushpin Studios, a much-lauded company that challenged many of the prevailing trends in graphic design thinking in the 1970s. He now has his own practice, Milton Glaser Inc. Richard Wilde has been chair of the advertising and design programmes at the School of Visual Arts in New York since the 1970s. He is a senior vice president at the Ryan Drossman Marc USA ad agency and also runs his own design company.

Bierut was not one of the signatories. He reported that while one of his partners in Pentagram, J. Abbott Miller, had signed the manifesto, another (Paula Scher) found it 'elitist and nonsense'. Glaser agreed to sign the manifesto only after an earlier draft had been modified: it was 'too polemical and not inclusive enough . . . it basically took a stand and . . . did not allow for any elasticity in who was admitted into the game. It sort of said "choose or die". . . . My feeling about it in general is if you don't give anybody anyplace to go, they don't pay any attention to you'.

Bierut made a telling distinction between the framing of the manifesto in *Adbusters* (a 'very absolutist view . . . sort of, sell your soul or bring capitalism to its knees') and his own position: it is 'simply asking for a shift in priorities as opposed to a complete disavowal of commercial work'. Even with these relatively modest aims in mind, Bierut sensed a certain degree of alienation among many readers of the manifesto largely because of the nature of the list of signatories (whom he referred to as the 'usual suspects'). In this context, he agreed that the purposes of the manifesto might have been better served by excluding signatures altogether, or at least employing 'a broader, more provocative list' of adherents. In sum, he suggested that, 'It remains to be seen whether that's an exclusionary, elitist position, taken by people who could afford to take it, as opposed to one that actually was tempting [designers] to cross over'.

Helfand, in contrast to Glaser, suggested that it is 'a call to order: this is not an industry in which you need to purify the practice, but there might be some basic understandings, some general context in which we can define the values we bring to our work'. Unlike Bierut, she also thought that having the manifesto signed by the 'usual suspects' (herself included) was actually one of its strengths: 'would this thing have gathered strength in numbers if fourteen thousand people [i.e. the entire AIGA membership] had signed it? That would have cancelled itself out as a special thing'. When I raised the possibility that the manifesto was simply preaching to the converted (since, in my view, advertising, not design, was the real target of the manifesto's scorn), Helfand responded that the kind of posturing in and around the manifesto was 'endemic to these kinds of tribal organizations. . . . the [AIGA] tribe gets together . . . and talks about design'. Indeed, she maintained that such activities were functional for anyone who had chosen design as a career: 'Years ago when I was a graphic designer at a newspaper and I was the only trained designer on a staff of five hundred journalists', it was 'incredibly therapeutic . . . I loved to go and gather with other designers and know that I was doing things right; there were other people that cared about things'. While the AIGA has clearly proved useful to Helfand as a source of support and camaraderie, she qualified this statement by noting that, 'The degree that that has any impact on culture at large is not so certain'. She expressed a hope that the manifesto might reach beyond 'the design ghetto' rather than 'support[ing] and advanc[ing] this kind of hierarchy and stratification, which may also have cultural precedent in all sorts of organizations'.

Glaser characterized the signatories as a 'cadre' who must continue to promote the ideas in the manifesto and encourage practical responses if it is to be of any consequence – 'otherwise any polemical statement will more or less go by the boards'. Glaser's more general view on matters of ethics was that 'there is an area of ambiguity about what is harmful, what is not, and so on'. Of the manifesto in particular, he said: 'certainly I agree with the fundamental issue, which is that one should try to do no harm, and to some extent that is the most attractive thing about a proposition of this sort'. Glaser was also pointedly philosophical about the role of designers:

> If you begin with the premise that what we work at more often than not involves to some degree a distortion or misrepresentation, it is very difficult to be at any point in this spectrum without having sinned. . . . the question really is how to balance the reality of professional life – and earning a living obviously – and one's desire not to cause harm.

Sagmeister suggested that one could distinguish between individuals for whom 'design plays a very crucial role in their life' and those for whom it is simply a nine-to-five occupation. The former group was typified by the signatories of First Things First and Sagmeister himself: 'I think it's great. If I'd been approached I'd definitely have done it, I would have signed it too. . . . Why would you want to be part of this incredible machinery that produces this amount of unbelievable junk?' Sagmeister's identification was with the 'gist' of the manifesto; in his elaboration of this point, it became clear that the 'junk' to which he referred is actually badly conceived and executed design work – comparable, perhaps, to advertising 'clutter'. During his well-attended talk at the AIGA conference in Las Vegas in 1999, he attributed this 'fluff' to a lack of political or even religious conviction on the part of designers.[16]

The Las Vegas event, the AIGA's eighth biennial conference, was attended by around 3,200 people, including 300 students. Bierut was charged with providing the closing comments for the event and, in light of this experience, he testified to the sheer range of responses to the manifesto that he had encountered within the first few weeks of its reemergence. Further, he noted what he called the 'inverse relationship' between the aesthetic theme of the conference ('America: Cult & Culture') and the ascetic tone of the manifesto. He also anticipated that the cumulative effect of the recent 'design boom' (the result of a strong economy) and the 'wretched excess' of Las Vegas itself might give designers pause for reflection. For this reason especially Bierut thought that the manifesto's appearance (particularly in *Adbusters*) was 'really interesting, really provocative and perhaps extremely timely'. Bierut praised *Adbusters* in particular for 'see[ing] design as an active tool in creating social change'. This he compared favourably – at least in principle – to the AIGA membership's aspirations, which he characterized as a 'universal' desire to have 'normal people' and the 'business community' alike 'know and care about design; to understand what it is and to know that it's important'.

Both Helfand and Bierut cited specific instances in their own day-to-day work that served to illustrate the difficulties of ethical practice. Helfand complained bitterly about the excesses of the marketers she works with:

> I'm sitting with thirty-five people in a conference room, and with a tremendous budget, and a tremendous amount of work and a tremendous set of expectations, and people aren't referred to as audiences, they're referred to as 'eyeballs'! How reductive and dehumanizing can that be? And yet, that's what they're thinking about: leveraging the knowledge they can get from market research to then go out and build their brand and get people to buy stuff. . . . I think designers have to think carefully about the role they play in that mix. I have clients who are asking me to do things, you know I have to think about it very carefully.

Bierut was remarkably candid about his own company's activities, noting that Pentagram has worked for 'all the big bad ones', as identified in what he called *Adbusters'* 'litany of must-to-avoid' companies, including Nike and Disney. He highlighted the ethical dilemmas of 'dirtying oneself in the muddy ponds of commercial practice' by repeating an anecdote he had shared with the audience at the AIGA conference about one of his 'most worthy' clients. According to Bierut, the Brooklyn Academy of Music has 'bravely put on interesting avant-garde performances', 'championed free expression, and really advanced the cause of culture . . . as well as reaching out to their community. . . . they've been great citizens of Brooklyn'. He added: 'they're a fantastic client. . . . they're a pleasure to work with, I'm very proud of the work I've done for them, and their biggest sponsor is Philip Morris'. Bierut then asked the pointed question, 'am I advancing the arts in America? Am I helping the underprivileged, arts-starved, and culture-starved Brooklyn community, or am I furnishing the ugly face of the makers of a product that kills thousands and thousands of people?'

Glaser anticipated this kind of conundrum when he noted that:

> designers *per se* are usually in a very weak position in regard to what they do; they don't make the determinations, they don't decide what is to be sold, they don't decide on the strategy or the objectives very often. They are, to a large extent, at the end of a long process where these essential decisions have been made by others. . . . Designers have to recognize that their role has become . . . a mediation between clients and an audience, where they act more like telephone lines than they do like initiators.

Glaser suggested that it is through this kind of realization that designers can come to a more grounded epiphany about the potential harm – or good – they can effect through their work practices. Helfand echoed the view that designers' hands are increasingly tied: in reference to her particular interest in ethical issues surrounding design and new media (including the development of websites, CD-ROMs, etc.) she said: 'the rules are being rewritten, but not by designers. . . . we're getting pushed into these roles where we're meant to visualize some fleeting information . . . giving form to content that's not thought through in any meaningful way'.

When asked if he felt some sense of *deja vu*, given his vast experience in the field – Glaser is a septuagenarian – he observed that

> at the end of every century in human history – not to mention the millennium itself – there's been this sense that the world is used up, that things have gone wrong, that the wrong people are in power, and that it's time for a fresh vision of reality. . . . it's linked in some way to the Arts and Crafts movement, the Viennese Secession, to Dadaism. All of these desires to clean up the act and to basically produce art or design that is socially responsible. Of course that occurs with great regularity, and that gets subsumed into the needs of the larger culture, to produce things to sell and to buy.

Was this any reason not to react to the manifesto?

> No, I don't think it makes it any less important. It actually shows a sense of historical continuity . . . what gets lost when people don't pay attention

to history. But it *has* to be said, because things have reached a point where, if it isn't said, all you can look forward to is an increasing lowering of human standards and sense of human community. This feeling that you could do anything to an audience as long as it sells the goods is oppressive.

Relative sinners: intermediaries on advertising vs. design

While Helfand, for example, saw First Things First as a community-building exercise for a business that did not need to change substantially, others, most notably Glaser, were more candid about the inevitability of 'sinning' at some stage in one's career. Glaser also noted that 'people in the advertising world certainly represent a more visible and more forceful expression of these ideas than what we find in the so-called world of design'. Indeed, advertising was repeatedly targeted, even scape-goated, for the ills identified in the manifesto – much to the frustration of Richard Wilde, for one. At the time I spoke to him, Wilde was only vaguely aware of the manifesto. After I sent him a copy, he remarked that while it looked good at first glance, ultimately he felt it was 'truly naïve' and 'high-handed'. He defended advertising's record by pointing out that, unlike designers, 'American ad agencies contribute 10% of their combined output to social issues, in the form of PSAs – or Public Service Announcements'.

As an indirect response to Glaser's suggestion that designers 'do no harm', Wilde said: 'who's to say what's good and what's not good? From where I sit I could take most any product and find real flaws'. Indeed, Wilde seemed to be the most conversant of my interviewees with regard to specific environmental and political issues beyond the immediate purview of design and advertising practice. Examples he readily cited included products made overseas through the use of exploitative labour practices, the use of carcinogenic chemicals to treat fruit and vegetables, aerosols and the production of leather goods. Ultimately, however, Wilde saw the strength of the manifesto in the fact that it 'opens up the question and gets people thinking and it gets their blood churned a little bit and it opens up debate; and debate on this is probably the single most important thing'.

According to First Things First's signatories, it is advertising's 'techniques and apparatus . . . [that] have persistently been presented to us as the most lucrative, effective and desirable use of our talents'. Andrew Howard has faulted the original manifesto, and Ken Garland in particular, for making unnecessary concessions to advertising. When Garland declared in a 1964 interview that '[we] are not against advertising as a whole' because '[t]he techniques of publicity and selling are vital to Western society' (quoted in Howard, 1994: 75), Howard suggested 'that what Garland is arguing for is the same cake, sliced differently', rather than 'a different cake altogether' (1994: 75). As it turns out, Garland has acknowledged that he has, over the ensuing years, 'had some qualms about the pragmatic flavour of that part of the manifesto' (Garland, 1994: 3), but maintains that the original concern of First Things First was 'spending priorities rather than social consciousness' (1994: 3).

Glaser thought that advertising people must be brought to the table although, for him, 'they have the most to lose'. However he also maintained that designers should not feel ethically superior to ad people or 'removed from the fray', since the issues for both camps are the same (never mind that, for designers, this 'is somewhat obscured by our loyalty to beauty, so called'). Bierut emphasized his belief that there is no way to make a clear-cut distinction between 'right' and 'wrong' in the design business and, further, that it is much harder to make ethical decisions in design than it is in advertising – mainly because the motives of the latter are, for him, singularly oriented towards commercial persuasion. In contrast, Helfand thought that 'intrinsically there's nothing wrong with advertising' – although she did feel that 'marketing might be [the enemy]'. Here she included activities such as market research, focus groups and brand-building.

In contrast to design, there seems to be something resolutely furtive or even confessional about the notion of ad people taking the time to criticize the workings of their own profession. While the rhetoric of advertising speaks tirelessly of subversion, resistance and revolution, its near-universal complicity in supporting the most fundamental tenets of capital accumulation perhaps serve to ensure that its practitioners remain – overtly at least – committed believers. A clue to this distinction lies in the paucity of venues for critical debate about advertising for its practitioners. There are isolated exceptions (e.g. Gossage, 1986; Lury, 1994; Helm, 2000) but perhaps because of the education and training that ad people generally receive, the critical insight offered by such rare contributions is most often particularly limited. Further, although the ad business has long supported the creation of public service announcements (PSAs) for various interest groups – drunk driving, anti-drugs, etc. – these rarely, if ever, take the messages or methods of advertising itself to task.

A public debate about First Things First was organized by the AIGA and held in New York in April 2000. Among the invited panelists were Jay Chiat, cofounder of Chiat/Day, one of the most successful and high-profile American ad agencies of recent years. He was unabashed about his own track record – Chiat/Day's emergent reputation was due in no small part to its work for Nike – and seemed indifferent to the palpable sense of urgency both at the debate and conveyed in the manifesto.

Another panelist, Kevin Lyons, was recently declared one of a 'bumper crop of remarkable young talents' in 2000's *ID* Forty Designers Under Thirty feature. He had declared in interview with *ID* that graphic design 'is a true guerilla art form'; if he was not a designer, he would be 'Doing guerilla activity of a different sort'. Further, he claimed that his work is 'informed by culture and politics'.

Lyons' clients include Nike, Stüssy and Urban Outfitters. At the debate, Lyons recounted how he had worked on campaigns conceived to persuade inner city youth to choose to buy Nike shoes. While this had the ring of a confessional, his tone was anything but. Indeed, there seemed to be something altogether absent in the contributions of Chiat and Lyons, a yawning gap between the earnestness of the manifesto and the possibility that their disclosures might somehow implicate them as targets of its criticism.

Discussion: fall-out from First Things First

First Things First has provoked a fair range of responses from 'name' designers and art directors. While sharing a largely unspecified commitment to social responsibility, reactions were varied among these intermediaries as to the perceived severity of the situation as described in the manifesto. Further, they seemed to feel that, at the limit, designers either had their hands tied or were simply innocent of the criticisms levelled at them (or were significantly less culpable than ad folk). More telling, perhaps, was the way in which the 'usual suspects' policed one another's level of involvement: in one or two cases it seemed that the politics of inclusion or exclusion as a signatory might actually outweigh the import of First Things First itself.

Since his interview with me, Bierut has taken a decidedly negative public position on the manifesto. In a recent article (Bierut, 2000) in *ID*, he set about criticizing the signatories of the manifesto partly because – with a few exceptions – they 'have specialized in [designing] extraordinarily beautiful things for the cultural elite, not the denizens of your local 7-Eleven' (Bierut, 2000: 76). Unlike his comments in interview, Bierut's somewhat glib response is characteristic of a tit-for-tat dialogue that has characterized much of the ensuing debate over First Things First. It is generally difficult to gauge whether individual responses have been borne of a genuine commitment to further discussion or have merely been symptomatic of a kind of turf wars played out in the pages of design magazines. To illustrate: two of the three responses to Bierut's article published in the letters page of the next issue of *ID* were from the editors of other design magazines. One was Steven Heller, editor of the *AIGA Journal of Graphic Design*; the other was Rudy VanderLans, editor of *Emigre*. Both were highly critical of Bierut's argument, with VanderLans accusing Bierut of working to 'maintain the status quo'.

On a more positive note, the letters page of the October/November 2000 issue of *Adbusters* carried a brief contribution from David Berman, National Ethics Chair of the Society of Graphic Designers of Canada. He reported that, after 'a passionate discussion' centring on the manifesto at a recent international design conference, 'the delegates unanimously agreed to sign the manifesto'. Furthermore,

> Unlike past signatories, this group only agreed to sign on if it were attached to a commitment to meaningful action. Each delegate agreed to perform at least one socially responsible project in their professional work this year, and we are setting up a way for publicly collecting and publicizing these acts as an inspiration for others.
>
> (Berman, 2000)

Berman was also chiefly responsible for the unprecedented development and implementation of a code of ethics for the Ontario chapter of the Society. Designers can now sit an exam to become Registered Graphic Designers (RGD), and Berman has high hopes that the initiative will be taken up by other chapters across Canada. In interview, Berman also said that it has received demonstrable support from the Ontario government, to the extent that it has begun specifying in some of its advertised contract work for the Province that only RGDs need apply.

Responses to First Things First have also been divided along generational lines. The public debate about the manifesto organized by the AIGA was held at the Fashion Institute of Technology, and was attended by many students – some of whom expressed puzzlement and even dismay at the panel's responses during the question and answer period. Discussions with educators at several educational institutions confirmed the degree to which young people have readily identified with the manifesto's criticisms. Elizabeth Resnick is a professor in the graphic design programme at Massachusetts College of Art, or MassArt. She also has a design practice and has long been an active member of the Boston chapter of the AIGA. In interview she was emphatic in noting that the reemergence of First Things First was highly significant for her students, strongly resonating with many of their formative concerns.

Katherine McCoy, during her long tenure as co-Chairman of the Department of Design at the Cranbrook Academy of Art, argued for the inclusion of 'issue-oriented work' (1994: 113) for design students to counter what she has termed the generally 'apolitical' nature of their educations. Indeed, this was very much part of McCoy's signature influence at Cranbrook. Similarly, the arrival of Sheila Levrant de Bretteville, a self-described 'graphic designer and public artist', as director of graduate studies in graphic design at Yale University's School of Art in 1990 also heralded a significant shift in pedagogical emphasis towards specifically *social* issues. Both McCoy and de Bretteville signed the First Things First manifesto. The most telling consequences of the return of the manifesto, then, may ultimately be measured through its impact on design education.

The Lasn–Dixon line: intermediaries as revolutionaries

One of the strongest advocates of the manifesto has been the Media Foundation, through its publication *Adbusters*. The magazine, which has historically fostered a blend of consumer and environmental activism, carries little or no advertising; in fact, it has become particularly well-known for its spoofs of prominent ad campaigns ('Absolut Impotence'; 'Joe Chemo'). Kalle Lasn, the editor of *Adbusters* (and cofounder of the Media Foundation) has recently elaborated a political agenda – both in the magazine and in book-form (Lasn, 1999b) – which he describes as 'culture jamming'.[17] It is through his elaborations on this strategy, and his utilization of the First Things First manifesto in particular, that Lasn continues to make overtures to both graphic designers and ad creatives:

> We are going to be the first activist movement to be launched by print ads and TV spots, by putting up billboards and by this more visual image-oriented thrust. In that sense, graphic artists are the cutting edge of what we are doing. Not only that, but I've found that graphic artists are in some sense the perfect people to launch a revolution because they have an open-mindedness that I don't find in other professions. Their skills can be used to sell soap, sneakers and Coca-Cola, but they can also be used to change the world. More and more visual artists are realizing this.
>
> (Lasn, in Poynor, 2000: 98).

As part of its ongoing, open invitation to readers to join in the cause of culture jamming, the Autumn 1999 issue also carried a call for entries for a 'Creative Resistance Contest': 'If you're a designer, filmmaker, ad agency team or digital artist, you have the skills to affect the issues that concern you. Adbusters needs your help to sell ideas, not products. Send us your best social marketing concept – storyboard, video, poster, print-ad, parody, installation or performance art piece. Create. Resist. Contest' (*Adbusters*, Autumn 1999: 63).

In gestures such as this, *Adbusters* may be acting as a bridge between critics and disillusioned ad people, at least according to its editor: 'there is a huge percentage of graphic artists within the advertising industry who are profoundly unhappy with their industry's ethical neutrality. Given the chance they would dearly love to be using their skills for other purposes, and these people finished up being very powerful allies for us' (quoted in Poynor, 1998: 40).

In interview with me, Lasn was full of enthusiasm for his project: with First Things First he hoped to 'launch a vigorous debate about why designers are sitting on the fence, and why they don't recognize the fact that they are actually foot-soldiers for consumer capitalism. . . . Designers are supporting a system that is unsustainable'. For the AIGA conference in Las Vegas, Lasn and Dixon recruited Jonathan Barnbrook, a well-known experimental typographer, to design a 48 ft billboard poster that was displayed outside the conference. Quoting the celebrated designer Tibor Kalman,[18] it read: 'Designers: Stay away from corporations that want you to lie for them'.

For Lasn, then, graphic design affords its practitioners the latitude to explore their dissent openly; so-called political graphics can, at least nominally, be accommodated as a legitimate form of design expression – as the *Adbusters* feature attests. (Tellingly, it is *Adbusters* alone that specifically refers to First Things First as a 'Design' manifesto.) It must also be said that Lasn, a former documentary film maker, and Dixon, the magazine's art director, are intermediaries in the rare position of being able to lead with their consciences: rather than supplement business-as-usual with prosocial gestures, they have been able to dedicate their entire efforts to the politics of media activism.

In the issue of *Adbusters* that preceded the relaunch of First Things First, Lasn wrote a scathing attack in which he elaborated on his conviction that 'culture jamming will become to our era what civil rights was to the '60s, what feminism was to the '70s, what environmental activism was to the '80s' ('The culture jammers network', *Adbusters* Autumn 1999: 80). In 'The New Activism', he declared that 'we're not feminists', 'we're not lefties', and 'we're not academics' (see also Lasn, 1999b). Among the shortcomings of these dubiously contrived – and apparently mutually exclusive – cohorts, were such crimes as 'communications professors who tell their students everything that's wrong with the world – and nothing about how to fix it'.[19]

When Edward Herman, co-author with Noam Chomsky of *Manufacturing Consent* (Herman and Chomsky, 1988), wrote in to complain that 'Lasn's effort to make culture jamming into a general philosophy and program of activism . . . is intellectually and programmatically pitiful' (Herman, 1999: 12), this was Lasn's accompanying reply – which is worth repeating *verbatim*: 'Once again, a traditional lefty describes as "action" such efforts as "thinking very hard" and writing proposals that others, presumably, are expected to carry forward. But what have you done lately besides talk and write, Mr. Herman? Would the left be in so sorry a state if it had permitted itself more action – even if "based on outrage"?' (Lasn, 1999a: 12)

Conclusion: towards a cultural economy of graphic design and advertising

In a short essay entitled 'All the world's a stage, screen or magazine: when culture is the logic of late capitalism', Angela McRobbie (1996) argues for the import-ance of studying 'the production of culture' and 'the sort of people who now work in culture, or who aspire to work in culture' (1996: 336). Further, McRobbie calls into question several undesirable trends that she detects within cultural studies as it has been practiced. These are tendencies towards 'overthe-orizing' and a 'confin[ement] . . . to the world of the text' – both of which can be understood, at least partially, as the result of 'fairly damning critiques of . . . empiricism, ethnography and the category of experience' (1996: 337). As I have tried to show, one way to work *against* the textualism to which I alluded at the beginning of this paper is to actively engage with McRobbie's 'three E's' (i.e. 'empiricism, ethnography and the category of experience').

In the introduction to his ethnographic study of the production of a documentary series about childhood for American public television, Barry Dornfeld (1998) states:

> An ethnographic approach to cultural production offers the possibility of rethinking and bridging the theoretical dichotomy between production and consumption, between producers' intentional meanings and audience members' interpreted meanings, and between production studies and reception studies.
>
> (1998: 12–13)

This sounds like an ambitious project indeed, but one that I believe can be achieved through the modest assertion that we could benefit from applying a cultural studies perspective to selected work cultures – sites that are responsible for generating the media and cultural texts that, in the rush to analysis, have been routinely disarticulated from their generative environments.

Furthermore, while we often treat the commercial media system as inherently counter-democratic, and, through its products and corporate policies, as an overwhelmingly conservative cultural force, we should recognize that this orientation is *institutional*: it will not suffice as a universal characterization of the system *and* all those who work in it. To the extent that we invest emancipatory potential in the subjective experiences of media audiences, so, too, we would do well to note the progressive (and, on occasion, radical) micro-currents at play within media organizations of all sizes. Very recent British field research on fashion designers (McRobbie, 1998, 2000), ad men (Nixon, 1997a, 1997b) and retail workers (du Gay, 1996), and the general development of a cultural economy perspective (du Gay, 1997), threaten to complicate a neat (and misleadingly held) binary opposition between homogenized productive forces on the one hand, and liberatory consumption practices on the other.

Studies such as these compare favourably with recent ethnographies of media practices in the USA, for example Henderson's (1995) research on film school, Lutz and Collins' (1993) investigation of the production and reception of *National Geographic* magazine, and Dornfeld (1998). As Dornfeld argues:

> We need to rethink producers as particular types of agents, producing media texts within contexts constrained by both culture, ideology, and economy, but operating within particular social locations and frameworks, not floating above society, as many approaches to the study of media forms seem to imply. This kind of reorientation would allow us to discuss with greater specificity and clarity the relationship between media forms and

practices and the larger public spheres they produce and are situated within.

(1998: 13)

By broadening the focus of critical attention in these ways we can continue to tease out the characteristic contours of the relationship between the subjective claims of designers and ad creatives and the structural constraints within which they generally operate; to explore the ways in which commercial practice enables non-commercial endeavours; and, to identify those subjective and/or structural elements that ultimately result in conservative, regressive or even pernicious 'texts'. Put bluntly, then: if graphics, ads and commercials are often so abundant in ideological cant, why not pay attention to the activities and beliefs of the highly skilled group that creates them – the cultural intermediaries – with the ultimate aim of training and using such talent more responsibly, and steering it toward more progressive ends?[20]

Finally, it is my contention that cultural economy, as a gesture or an intervention (for it is surely too early to call it a theory) holds the promise of opening up a critical space in which to further develop our understanding of the intermediaries and, by extension, contemporary culture.

Notes

1   Definitions of the term 'graphic design' vary considerably. Until very recently it was also entirely absent from most major dictionaries (Wheeler, 1997). The *de facto* reference for graphic design students, critics and historians – Philip B. Meggs' *A History of Graphic Design* (Meggs, 1998) – begins its ambitious survey with the cave paintings of Lascaux. There is relative consensus, however, that the term itself was first used by W. A. Dwiggins in 1922 to describe an emergent set of practices that grew out of 'commercial art' (now more familiar as the practice of advertising).

2   The elaboration of Bourdieu's terms of analysis has been disappointingly thin. For exceptions, see Nixon (1997b), du Gay *et al.* (1997), and Stevens (1998). The latter employs Bourdieu's notions of taste, class and habitus to examine the rarefied world of distinguished architects. Aside from its decidedly polemical premises, Stevens' study offers some useful pointers for exploring the idea that individual success in graphic design is not simply premised on exceptional talent, but is also partly the result of accumulated cultural capital (including formative involvement with already-distinguished designers).

3   While Marilyn Crafton Smith (1994) has laid out a basic argument for a cultural studies approach to graphic design criticism, my intention here is actually to challenge this received model of cultural studies, or at least the bulk of research and analysis on advertising and design generated in its name.

4   This is not to discount certain ongoing debates that are often confined to the

design community and its most immediate academic counterparts. For example: the marginalization of women (e.g. Buckley, 1989; Thomson, 1994) and African-Americans (Margolin, 2000) in graphic design history; the role of an engaged politics of social activism (e.g. Lupton, 1999; McCoy, 1994); and, the possibilities for a radically improved professional milieu of social responsibility (e.g. van Toorn, 1998; ten Duis & Haase, 1999). 1989 also saw the advent of *Dangerous Ideas*, AIGA's third national conference, which ultimately proved to be a factor in emergent debates about social responsibility in graphic design. It featured Stuart Ewen as keynote speaker, but is perhaps best remembered for a heated debate between two well-known designers, sparked by one citing the other's company as an example of dubious business practices (see Brown (1989) and 'Tibor Kalman vs. Joe Duffy', *Print*, March/April 1990, pp. 68–75, 158–63).

5   The American Institute of Graphic Arts is a professional organization for art directors and designers with a national membership in excess of 14,000. With an administrative centre in New York, it has over 40 chapters throughout the United States.

6   *ID* was originally called *Industrial Design*, but has long since expanded its editorial focus to include all manner of two- and three-dimensional designed objects and spaces. Not to be confused with the British style magazine *i-D*.

7   Renamed *Trace: AIGA Journal of Design* in 2001. *Trace* ceased publication after three issues as a result of cost-cutting measures taken by the AIGA in the wake of the events of September 11, 2001.

8   *Critique* ceased publication in 2000.

9   *Emigre* has recently returned to an editorial focus on music.

10   A potential caveat with these publications, however, is the marked tendency to rely on the same small pool of writers. Indeed, there is often such a degree of familiarity among the participants that entire conversations seem to take place through articles, qualifications, expansions, and rebuttals, from month to month across a very small number of magazines and journals.

11   This is aside from scholarly publications such as the journal *Design Issues* (see also Margolin and Buchanan (1995) and Doordan (1995) for collected essays from this periodical) and the three-part special issue of the journal *Visible Language* edited by Andrew Blauvelt (1994/95). Limitations of space have prevented me from fully exploring these contributions here.

12   The AIGA held an event on First Things First shortly after the manifesto reappeared, and, more recently, organized a two-day conference on design history and criticism called *Looking Closer*. The 2001 AIGA national conference, to be held in Washington DC in September, aimed to address design's place in a broader social, political and cultural context. (The conference was ultimately postponed until March 2002 due to the events of September 11, 2001.) Academic interest has also begun to grow: see for example the conferences *Democratic Communications in a Branded World*, Carleton University (Ottawa, May 2001), and *Declarations of [inter]dependence and the im[media]cy of design*, Concordia University (Montreal, October 2001).

13   Some of these were originally conducted for an article in the *AIGA Journal of Graphic Design* (Soar, 1999). Permissions were obtained at the time to re-use the material in scholarly endeavors.

14   My emphasis on distinguished, or 'name', designers presents specific problems, not least of which is the temptation to use this evidence to generalize to the entire membership of AIGA, and beyond. Stevens (1998) provides a useful critique of the star system in architecture, in which he suggests that the achievement of distinction has a great deal to do with having the right class background, education, and formative professional connections.

15   Glaser has, in the past, taken a principled stand against unethical business practices. See, for example, his orchestrated withdrawal from a design competition organized by Chrysler (Glaser, 1997). He had discovered that the car company had instituted a policy of insisting on approving editorial copy in magazines before agreeing to buy advertising in them. Glaser persuaded fellow nominee Steven Heller, and jurors Jessica Helfand and Tibor Kalman, to join in his protest. Kalman, who had won the award the previous year, 'offered to give his $10,000 award to charity or to use it to fight publicly this nasty form of censorship'.

16   Sagmeister noted, approvingly, that the designer of the much-lauded film titles for the movie *Seven* (1995, Dir. David Fincher, New Line Cinema) is a born-again Christian. He felt that the designer's 'very strong view on evil . . . [was] a point of departure. . . . I'm not a religious person but it . . . showed me that he has a strong backbone . . . and that's where it comes from'.

17   According to Rick Poynor, the term was 'coined in 1984 by the American experimental music and art collective, Negativland, to describe billboard liberation and other forms of media banditry' (Poynor, 1998: 39). See also Dery (1993) and Lasn (1999b).

18   Kalman, who died in 1999, was well-known in the design community for his outspoken views on design and social responsibility.

19   The fact that *Adbusters* has also featured articles by Professors Stuart Ewen, Mark Crispin Miller, and Sut Jhally – not to mention *homages* to the trenchant critiques of Barbara Kruger and *Ms.* magazine, seems altogether puzzling.

20   While this can be achieved most immediately through more enlightened decisions about which clients to take on and the working relationships so developed, it also has much to do with creative execution, such as the selection of specific images to communicate a particular issue. Lavin (2001), for example, argues that the abortion debate might be lifted out of its current rancorous deadlock – 'the pro-life helpless fetus versus the pro-choice helpless woman' (Lavin, 2001: 145) – through a conscious expansion of the range of images used in the designed communications (e.g. posters and leaflets) produced by both sides.

References

[. . .] (2000) 'Number of periodicals over time' and 'Number of periodicals over space', [. . .] 1, 53.

Adbusters (1999) 'Creative resistance contest', *Adbusters*, 27: 63.

Berman, D. (2000) [Letter to the editor] *Adbusters*, 32, Oct/Nov: 9.

Bierut, M. (2000) 'A manifesto with ten footnotes', *ID*, Mar/Apr, 76–8.

Bierut, M., Drenttel, W., Heller, S. and Holland, D. K. (eds) (1994) *Looking Closer: Critical Writings on Graphic Design*. New York: Allworth Press.

Bierut, M., Drenttel, W., Heller, S. and Holland, D. K. (eds) (1997) *Looking Closer 2: Critical Writings on Graphic Design*. New York: Allworth Press.

Bierut, M., Helfand, J., Heller, S. and Poynor, R. (eds) (1999) *Looking Closer 3: Classic Writings on Graphic Design*. New York: Allworth Press.

Blauvelt, A. (ed.) (1994/95) 'New perspectives: critical histories of graphic design', *Visible Language*, 28(3), 28(4), 29(1).

Bourdieu, P. (1984) *Distinction: A Social Critique of the Judgement of Taste*, trans. R. Nice. London: Routledge & Kegan Paul.

Brown, P. L. (1989) 'The media business: advertising; Designers worry about self-image', *The New York Times*, 12 October, D23.

Buchanan, R. (1998) 'Branzi's dilemma: design in contemporary culture', *Design Issues*, 14(1), 1–22.

Buckley, C. (1989) 'Made in patriarchy: toward a feminist analysis of women and design'. In V. Margolin (ed.) *Design Discourse*. Chicago: University of Chicago Press, pp. 251–64.

Dery, M. (1993) *Culture Jamming: Hacking, Slashing, and Sniping in the Empire of Signs*. Westfield, NJ: Open Magazine Pamphlet Series.

Doordan, D. (ed.) (1995) *Design History: An Anthology*. Cambridge, MA: MIT Press.

Dornfeld, B. (1998) *Producing Public Television, Producing Public Culture*. Princeton NJ: Princeton University Press.

du Gay, P. (1996) *Consumption and Identity at Work*. London: Sage.

du Gay, P. (ed.) (1997) *Production of Culture/Cultures of Production*. London: Sage/Open University.

du Gay, P., Hall, S., Janes, L., Mackay, H. and Negus, K. (1997) *Doing Cultural Studies: The Story of the Sony Walkman*. London: Sage/Open University.

Garland, K. (1994) 'First things last'. Letter to the editor, *Eye*, 14: 3.

Glaser, M. (1997) 'Censorious advertising', *The Nation*, 22 September: 7.

——— (2000) *Art is Work: Graphic Design, Interiors, Objects and Illustration*. Woodstock, NY: Overlook Press.

Gossage, H. (1986) *Is There any Hope for Advertising?* Urbana: University of Illinois.

Hall, P. and Sagmeister, S. (2001) *Sagmeister: Made you Look*. London: Booth-Clibborn Editions.

Helfand, J. (1998) *Paul Rand: American Modernist: Two Essays*.

Heller, S. and Finamore, M. (eds) (1997) *Design Culture: An Anthology of Writing from the AIGA Journal of Graphic Design*. New York: Allworth Press.

Helm, J. (2000) 'Saving advertising'. *Emigre*, 53, 4–20.

Henderson, L. (1995) 'Directorial intention and persona in film school', in L. Gross (ed.) *On the Margins of Art Worlds*. Boulder: Westview Press, pp. 149–66.

Herman, E. (1999) 'The new activism'. Letter to the editor, *Adbusters*, 27: 12.

Herman, E. and Chomsky, N. (1988) *Manufacturing Consent: The Political Economy of the Mass Media*. New York: Pantheon.

Howard, A. (1994) 'There is such a thing as society'. *Eye*, 13: 72–7.

Johnson, R. (1986/87) 'What is cultural studies anyway?'. *Social Text*, 16: 38–80.

Kalman, T., Hall, P. and Bierut, M. (1998) *Tibor Kalman, Perverse Optimist*. New York: Princeton Architectural Press.

Lasn, K. (1999a) Letters page. *Adbusters*, 27: 12.

—— (1999b) *Culture Jam: The Uncooling of America*^{TM}. New York: Eagle Brook/William Morrow.

Lavin, M. (2001) *Clean New World: Culture, Politics, and Graphic Design*. Cambridge, MA: MIT Press.

Lupton, E. (1999) 'Graphic design in the urban landscape', in J. Rothschild (ed.) *Design and Feminism: Re-visioning Spaces, Places, and Everyday Things*. New Brunswick: Rutgers University Press, pp. 57–65.

Lury, A. (1994) 'Advertising: moving beyond the stereotypes', in R. Keat, N. Whiteley and N. Abercrombie (eds) *The Authority of the Consumer*. London: Routledge.

Lutz, C. and Collins, J. (1993) *Reading National Geographic*. Chicago: University of Chicago Press.

Margolin, V. (2000) 'African-American designers in Chicago: some preliminary findings'. *AIGA Journal of Graphic Design*, 18(1): 9–10.

Margolin, V. and Buchanan, R. (1995) *The Idea of Design: A Design Issues Reader*. Cambridge, MA: MIT Press.

McCoy, K. (1994) 'Countering the tradition of the apolitical designer', in J. Myerson (ed.) *Design Renaissance: Selected Papers from the International Design Congress, Glasgow, Scotland 1993*. Horsham: Open Eye, pp. 105–14.

McRobbie, A. (1996) 'All the world's a stage, screen or magazine: when culture is the logic of late capitalism'. *Media, Culture & Society*, 18: 335–42.

—— (1998) *British Fashion Design: Rag Trade or Image Industry?* London: Routledge.

—— (2000) 'The return to cultural production: Case study, fashion journalism'. Conference paper, *Cultural economy workshop*, Open University.

Meggs, P. B. (1998) *A History of Graphic Design*, 3rd edn. New York: John Wiley & Sons.

Nixon, S. (1997a) 'Advertising executives as modern men: masculinity and the UK advertising industry in the 1980s', in M. Nava *et al.* (eds) *Buy this Book: Studies in Advertising and Consumption*. London: Routledge, pp. 103–19.

—— (1997b) 'Circulating culture', in P. du Gay (ed.) *Production of Culture/Cultures of Production*. London: Sage/Open University, pp. 177–220.

Poynor, R. (1998) 'Design is advertising, Part 2'. *Eye*, 30: 36–43.

—— (1999) 'First Things First: A brief history'. *Adbusters*, 27: 54–6.

—— (2000) 'Kalle Lasn: Ad buster'. *Graphis*, 325: 96–101.

Poynor, R. and Rock, M. (1995) 'What is this thing called graphic design criticism?'.
    Eye, 16: 56–9.
Smith, M. C. (1994) 'Culture is the limit: Pushing the boundaries of graphic design
    criticism and practice', *Visible Language*, 28(4): 298–316.
Soar, M. (1999) 'The impotence of being earnest'. *AIGA Journal of Graphic Design*,
    17(3): 6–7.
—— (2000) 'Encoding advertisements: ideology and meaning in advertising pro-
    duction'. *Mass Communication & Society*, 3(5): 415–37.
Stevens, G. (1998) *The Favored Circle: The Social Foundations of Architectural Distinction*.
    Cambridge, MA: MIT Press.
ten Duis, L. and Haase, A. (1999) *De wereld moe(s)t anders: Grafisch ontwerpen en
    idealism / The World Must Change: Graphic Design and Idealism [Sandberg Publication
    No. 18]*. Amsterdam: Sandberg Instituut/De Balie.
Thomson, E. M. (1994) 'Alms for oblivion: the history of women in early American
    graphic design'. *Design Issues*, 10(2): 27–48.
Wheeler, A. (1997) 'If it's not in the dictionary, it's not a real word', in S. Heller and
    M. Finamore (eds) *Design Culture: An Anthology of Writing from the AIGA Journal
    of Graphic Design*. New York: Allworth Press, pp. 84–5.
van Toorn, J. (1998) *Design beyond Design: Critical Reflection and the Practice of Visual
    Communication*. Maastricht: Jan Van Eyck Akademie.

Appendix

FIRST THINGS FIRST MANIFEST 2000

We, the undersigned, are graphic designers, art directors and visual communicators who have been raised in a world in which the techniques and apparatus of advertising have persistently been presented to us as the most lucrative, effective and desirable use of our talents. Many design teachers and mentors promote this belief; the market rewards it; a tide of books and publications reinforces it.

Encouraged in this direction, designers then apply their skill and imagination to sell dog biscuits, designer coffee, diamonds, detergents, hair gel, cigarettes, credit cards, sneakers, butt toners, light beer and heavy-duty recreational vehicles. Commercial work has always paid the bills, but many graphic designers have now let it become, in large measure, *what graphic designers do*. This, in turn, is how the world perceives design. The profession's time and energy is used up manufacturing demand for things that are inessential at best.

Many of us have grown increasingly uncomfortable with this view of design. Designers who devote their efforts primarily to advertising, marketing and brand development are supporting, and implicitly endorsing, a mental environment so saturated with commercial messages that it is changing the very way citizen-consumers speak, think, feel, respond and interact. To some extent we are all helping draft a reductive and immeasurably harmful code of public discourse.

There are pursuits more worthy of our problem-solving skills. Unprecedented environmental, social and cultural crises demand our attention. Many cultural interventions, social marketing campaigns, books, magazines, exhibitions, educational tools, television programs, films, charitable causes and other information design projects urgently require our expertise and help.

We propose a reversal of priorities in favor of more useful, lasting and democratic forms of communication — a mindshift away from product marketing and toward the exploration and production of a new kind of meaning. The scope of debate is shrinking; it must expand. Consumerism is running uncontested; it must be challenged by other perspectives expressed, in part, through the visual languages and resources of design.

In 1964, 22 visual communicators signed the original call for our skills to be put to worthwhile use. With the explosive growth of global commercial culture, their message has only grown more urgent. Today, we renew their manifesto in expectation that no more decades will pass before it is taken to heart.

Jonathan Barnbrook
Nick Bell
Andrew Blauvelt
Hans Bockting
Irma Boom
Sheila Levrant de Bretteville
Max Bruinsma
Siân Cook
Linda van Deursen
Chris Dixon
William Drenttel
Gert Dumbar
Simon Esterson
Vince Frost
Ken Garland
Milton Glaser
Jessica Helfand
Steven Heller
Andrew Howard
Tibor Kalman
Jeffery Keedy
Zuzana Licko
Ellen Lupton
Katherine McCoy
Armand Mevis
J. Abbott Miller
Rick Poynor
Lucienne Roberts
Erik Spiekermann
Jan van Toorn
Teal Triggs
Rudy VanderLans
Bob Wilkinson

Reproduced courtesy of Adbusters Media Foundation.

Routledge
Taylor & Francis Group

■   Book Review

Catherine Johnson
WORKING THROUGH TELEVISION

John Ellis, *Seeing Things: Television in the Age of Uncertainty* (London: I. B. Tauris, 2000), 193 pp., ISBN 1-86064-125-3 Hbk, £35.00, ISBN 1-86064-489-9 Pbk, £12.95.

As we enter a new millennium, the question 'what is television studies?' has provoked a number of renewed 'post-millennial' attempts to define both the discipline and the medium.[1] Much of this academic interest stems from two associated concerns. The first revolves around the instability of television studies within the academy and the inconsistency of approaches towards a subject that is dispersed across so many different disciplines. The second arises from the not unrelated recognition that the medium of television itself is undergoing a phenomenal shift, which challenges the conceptual frameworks within which it has been theorized. John Ellis' *Seeing Things: Television in the Age of Uncertainty*, as its title suggests, is a way of 'coming to terms with television' (p. 3) in this era of change.

Ellis develops two interrelated concepts for theorizing the specificity of television as a medium: 'witness' and 'working through'. Developed in the opening chapters, 'witness' provides a way of thinking about what Ellis regards as a fundamental shift in perception brought about by television's live and intimate mode of address. Situated within the rituals of domestic life and imbued with the sense of being co-present with its audience even when it moves away from a predominantly live mode of production, Ellis argues that television brings us into contact with the world in a way that engenders a sense of powerless knowledge, through which 'we cannot say that we do not know' (p. 1). This experience of witness is dealt with by television through the process of 'working through' explored in the second section of the book. Developed from the psychoanalytic term whereby patients work through a major revelation until it is exhausted, 'working through' describes what Ellis sees as television's primary social function, as a 'vast mechanism for processing the material of the witnessed world into more narrativized, explained forms' (p. 78).

Ellis historicizes this analysis of the specificity of television by examining the development of the medium over three distinct eras: scarcity, availability and plenty. Chapter 4 explores television's development as a key component of consumer society in an era of scarcity characterized by the relatively small number of channels and broadcasters. It is the shifts in the growth of satellite and cable in the late 1970s and early 1980s that lead into the second era – of availability. As its name suggests, this is the moment in which television services are expanded, and the majority of Ellis' book is concerned with exploring the process of 'working through' in this era. In particular, he provides some interesting theoretical and practical insights into the shifting notion of scheduling, as well as a less satisfying gloss over the fortunes of the primary television genres. In his final

Cultural Studies ISSN 0950-2386 print/ISSN 1466-4348 online © 2002 Taylor & Francis Ltd
http://www.tandf.co.uk/journals/routledge/09502386.html
DOI: 10.1080/09502380210142805

chapter, Ellis argues that a new television era is about to emerge, the age of plenty, which threatens to fundamentally alter the pre-existing patterns and experiences of broadcasting.

On the whole, this is an interesting, insightful and very readable attempt to engage theoretically with the current upheaval in television and television studies. However, *Seeing Things* does suffer from its wide remit. It is questionable whether a medium as expansive and indeterminate as television can be fully accounted for through the concepts of witness and working through. 'Working through' is particularly problematic as a way of thinking about either the specificity of television, or its social function. Developed primarily in relation to factual broadcasting, its applicability to fictional television and the increasing number of hybrid genres remains rather disappointingly undertheorized. There is little space in Ellis' model for a consideration of pleasure, and his emphasis on the videographic over the cinematic in his discussion of Caldwell's *Televisuality* (consistently misspelt as 'Caudwell') seems symptomatic of his focus on non-illusionistic modes of representation. Perhaps more problematic than this is the neutrality of the term 'working through' which, in its transference from psychoanalysis, is constructed as an implicitly positive process. This obscures questions of power, making it a rather functionalist and politically neutral means of theorizing television's social role.

While Ellis does provide a historically sensitive discussion of television's social function, his model is steeped in the presumptions and ideologies of British public service television. This is most overt in the final chapter, in which Ellis mounts a defence of the British public service broadcasting model, rather than fully exploring the complexity of the multiple discourses and fragmentation envisaged both in television and in wider society in the imminent era of plenty. Throughout, Ellis fails to address the ways in which television's social function (and the processes of working through and witness) can be understood as nationally and industrially specific. As a consequence, his analysis tends to flatten out national differences, and Ellis' own nationally embedded position, as a British academic and practitioner, remains obscured.

However, although Ellis' theoretical model may not be entirely successful, his periodization is particularly useful. Although primarily applicable to Western television broadcasting, it provides a framework for thinking about the national and global implications of the industrial and technological shifts in television production. As such, Ellis opens the space for comparative analyses that address the impact of the increasingly international nature of television broadcasting on the production and consumption of nationally specific programmes. In addition to being of interest to those engaged in historical, industrial and social television research, *Seeing Things* will also be a valuable text for introducing students to the study of the historical shifts in television production and consumption, as well as providing them with an engaging theorization of television's social function.

Note

1   See, for example, Corner (1999), in particular the final chapter, and the research stemming from the Economic and Social Research Council's Media Economics and Media Culture Research Programme. In particular, Simon

Frith's evaluation of the disparate state of television studies, which argues for dialogue across the different strands of the discipline (2000) and Born's response, which proposes that 'television research should be reconnected to a sociology of culture' (2000: 405).

References

Born, Georgina (2000) 'Inside television: television studies and the sociology of culture', *Screen*, 41(4): 404–24.

Corner, John (1999) *Critical Ideas in Television Studies*. Oxford: Oxford University Press.

Frith, Simon (2000) 'The black box: the value of television and the future of television research', *Screen*, 41 (1): 33–50.

Routledge
Taylor & Francis Group

Notes on contributors

Paul du Gay is sub-Dean Research and attached to the Department of Sociology, Open University, UK. He is author of *Consumption and Identity at Work* (Sage, 1996) and *In Praise of Bureaucracy, Weber, Organization, Ethics* (Sage, 2000).

Catherine Johnson is researching a PhD on television fantasy at the University of Warwick. She has published on factual entertainment in the *European Journal of Cultural Studies*, 4 (1), February 2001, and has an article on the 1950s *Quatermass* serials forthcoming in *Small Screen, Big Ideas: Television in the 1950s* (Janet Thumim (ed.), I. B. Tauris, 2001).

Liz McFall teaches in the Department of Sociology at the Open University, UK. Amongst her recent articles is 'Typographical tricks and mundane effects: using the production context to reconsider the persuasiveness of nineteenth century advertising', in Paul du Gay and Michael Pryke (eds) *Cultural Economy* (Sage, 2001).

Angela McRobbie teaches in the Department of Media and Communication Studies, Goldsmith's College, University of London, UK, and is author of many books including *British Fashion Design, Rag Trade or Image Industry?* (Routledge, 1998).

Keith Negus teaches in the Department of Media and Communication Studies, Goldsmith's College, University of London, UK, and is author of *Producing Pop* (Edward Arnold, 1992), *Popular Music in Theory* (Polity Press, 1996) and *Music Genres and Corporate Cultures* (Routledge, 1999).

Sean Nixon teaches in the Department of Sociology, University of Essex, UK and is author of *Hard Looks, Masculinities, Spectatorship and Contemporary Consumption* (UCL Press & St Martin's Press, 1996) and *Creative Cultures, Gender and Creativity at Work in Advertising* (Sage, forthcoming).

Lise Skov is a cultural sociologist doing research on fashion in East Asia. She is the co-editor of *Women, Media and Consumption in Japan* (Curzon, 1995). She is currently teaching at the Southern Danish University, Denmark.

Matt Soar is visiting Assistant Professor of Video and Media Studies, School of Humanities, Arts and Cultural Studies, Hampshire College, USA.

Cultural Studies ISSN 0950-2386 print/ISSN 1466-4348 online © 2002 Taylor & Francis Ltd
http://www.tandf.co.uk/journals
DOI: 10.1080/09502380210139133

Routledge
Taylor & Francis Group

A note of thanks

The editors, staff, and publisher of *Cultural Studies* would like to extend their most sincere gratitude to Rachel Hall for her five year service to the journal; and for her commitment to and diligence in keeping the journal operations running smoothly. Rachel is currently completing her dissertation at the University of North Carolina, Chapel Hill. We wish her continued success in her pursuits.

Cultural Studies ISSN 0950-2386 print/ISSN 1466-4348 online © 2002 Taylor & Francis Ltd
http://www.tandf.co.uk/journals
DOI: 10.1080/0950238022000035722

CULTURAL STUDIES 16(4) 2002, 598–601

Routledge
Taylor & Francis Group

Notes for contributors

Submission

Authors should submit three complete copies of their paper, including any original illustrations to:

Prof Lawrence Grossberg and Della Pollock, Editors of *Cultural Studies*, Department of Communication Studies, CB#3285, 115 Bingham Hall, University of North Carolina at Chapel Hill, Chapel Hill, NC 27599–3285, USA; e-mail: cs-journ@email.unc.edu

It will be assumed that the author has retained a copy of his or her paper. Submission of a paper to *Cultural Studies* will be taken to imply that it presents original, unpublished work not under consideration for publication elsewhere. In submitting a manuscript the authors agree that the exclusive rights to reproduce and distribute the article have been given to the publishers. This includes reprints, photographic reproductions, microfilm, or any other reproduction of similar nature and translations, though copyright is retained by the author.

Manuscript format

All submissions should be in English, typed or computer printed in double spacing on one side of the paper only. Please include an abstract of up to 300 words (including 6 keywords) for purposes of review. The authors name should not appear anywhere on the manuscript except for on a detachable cover page along with an address, short biographical not and the title. Please supply and e-mail address if you have one and a contact number.

Photographs, tables and figures

Photographs should be high contrast black and white glossy prints. Tables and figures need not be rendered professionally but should be neatly drawn in black

udies ISSN 0950-2386 print/ISSN 1466-4348 online © 2002 Taylor & Francis Ltd
http://www.tandf.co.uk/journals

Copyright-protected material

Written permission to reproduce photographs, tables, figures, song lyrics or any other copyright protected material must be obtained by authors from the copyright-holders before submission.

Citation style

Manuscripts must conform to the Havard reference style. When an author's name is mentioned in the text, the date alone is inserted in parentheses immediately after the name: Smith (1970). When a less direct reference is made the name and date are given together in parentheses. Several authors are seperated by a semicolon: (Smith, 1970; Mbene, 1984).

When the reference is to dual or multiple authorship use: Smith and Jones (1971) for two authors and; Smith *et al.* for more than two. Only use initials if two authors have the same surname: (Smith, A., 1970; Smith, B., 1971).

If two or more works by the same author are cited for the same year, add lower case letters after the date to distinguish them: (Smith, 1970a, 1970b).

When using a republished book, a translation or a modern edition of an older book, give the date of the original publication as well: Smith (1970/1999). When using a reprinted article, cite the date of the original publication only.

When referring to mass media materials, include relevant information within parentheses: (Women's weekly, 16 July 1983: 32).

Treat recorded music as a book: the musician or group is the author, the title is underlined and the distributor is listed as the publisher;; treat television series and films similarly. Treat television episodes, poems, songs and short stories (i.e. works that are not usually published separately) as articles, placing the title in single quotation marks.

Reference List

Submissions should include a reference list conforming to the style shown in the following examples:

Book
Leach, Edmund (1976) *Culture and Communication*. Cambridge: Cambridge University Press.
Two or more references to the same author
Leach, Edmund (1976) *Culture and Communication*. Cambridge: Cambridge University Press.
— (1974) Levi-Strauss. London: Fontana.

Multiple authors
Ogden, C. G. and Richards, I. A. (1949) *The Meaning of Meaning* (2nd edn). London:
    Routledge and Kegan Paul.
Two references published in the same year; translated text; two places of publication
Lacan, Jacques (1977a) *Ecrits: A Selection*. Trans. Alan Sheridan. New York and
    London: Norton. (Originally published 1966).
Article in reader not already cited; multi volume work; article in book by same author
Leavis, F. R. (1945) "Thought' and Emotional Quality'. In his (ed.) (1968) *A Selec-
    tion from Scrutiny* (vol. 1). Cambridge: Cambridge University Press, 211–30.
Article in journal
Macherey, Pierre and Balibar, Etienne (1978) 'Literature as an ideological form:
    some Marxist propositions'. *Oxford Literary Review*, 3(1) 4–12.
Article in magazine or newspaper
Burstall, Tim (1977) 'Triumph and disaster for Australian films'. *The Bulletin*, 24 Sep-
    tember 1977: 45–54.
Film or TV programme
The War Game (1966). Dir. Peter Watkins, BBC.

Proofs

Page proofs will be sent for correction to the author whose name appears first
on the title page of the article unless otherwise requested. The difficulty and
expense involved in making amendments at this stage make it essential to prepare
their typescripts carefully: any alteration to the original text is strongly discour-
aged. The proofs should be returned as quickly as possible.

Offprints

Twenty five offprints and a copy of the issue in which the article appears will be
supplied free of charge to the author. There is no remuneration for publication
in *Cultural Studies*.

Guidelines for Book Reviews

Cultural Studies publishes reviews of current books that are of potential interest
to the journal's main audience: i.e., an international readership of scholars,
students, activists, and cultural workers interested in cultural studies (broadly
defined). Given the cross/multi-disciplinary nature of the journal's focus, reviews
should focus specifically on the relevance of the book(s) in question to cultural
studies (rather than to either the author's or the reviewer's 'home' discipline).

Completed reviews should be concise – i.e., 1000 words or less – and carefully proofread. External citations and endnotes do count against your word limit, so use them sparingly (if at all). Your review should include:

Heading information:
- Your name
- Title of the book review (short, preferably 5–6 words)
- Publication information: book author(s)/editor(s), book title, city/cities, publisher, date, page count, ISBN number and price for cloth/hardback, ISBN number and price for paperback.

Body of review:
- Brief description or explanation of the book's contents
- Discussion of the book's relevance to cultural studies
- Critical engagement with and assessment of the book's contents

Other information (on separate page):
- Word count of your review (excluding the heading information)
- Brief biographical note for the reviewer (2–3 lines)
- Your address/contact information (including phone number(s) and e-mail address)

General formatting guidelines:
- Reviews should be written in English and adhere to the journal's usual style guidelines (i.e., Harvard style).
- Reviews should be submitted in one of the following formats: WordPerfect (version 9.0 or earlier), Microsoft Word (2000 or earlier), or RTF (Rich Text Format).
- Reviews should be submitted either as an e-mail file attachment or on an IBM-compatible 3.5' floppy disk to one of the book review editors:

Stuart Price, School of Arts, de Montford University, The Gateway, Leicester LE1 9BH, UK; Ien Ang, Institute for Cultural Research, University of Western Sydney, Parramatta Campus, BCRI Building LZ, Locked Bag 1797, Penrith South DC NSW 1797, Australia; Alvaro Pina, Rua Jose P.Chaves, 6–3 Dto, 1500–377 Lisboa, Portugal; Gil Rodman, Department of Communication, University of South Florida, 4202 East Fowler Avenue, CIS 1040, Tampa, FL 33620–7800, USA.

BOMBAY—LONDON—NEW YORK

Amitava Kumar

"This is a work of luminous imagination and tenderness. Amitava Kumar is a startling story teller: that rare cultural critic who writes from and for the heart."

—Rob Nixon, University of Wisconsin

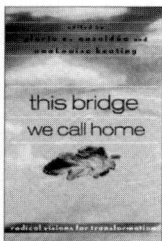

this bridge we call home
radical visions for transformation

Edited by anaLouise keating and gloria e. anzaldúa

More than twenty years after the ground-breaking anthology *This Bridge Called My Back* gloria e. anzaldúa and anaLouise keating have painstakingly assembled a new collection of over eighty original writings that offers a bold new vision of women-of-color consciousness for the twenty-first century.

QUOTATION MARKS

Marjorie Garber

Written with characteristic verve, *Quotation Marks* considers, among other subjects, how we depend upon the most quotable men and women in history, using great writers to bolster what we ourselves have to say.

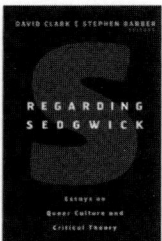

REGARDING SEDGWICK
Essays on Critical Theory and Queer Culture

Edited by David Clark and Stephen Barber

"The power, range, and immense utility of Eve Kosofsky Sedgwick's restlessly evolving, always surprising work are put on conspicuous display by the many different kinds of writing brought together in this experimental collection."

—David M. Halperin

THE CULTURE OF CAPITAL
Property, Cities, and Knowledge in Early Modern England

Henry Turner

Leading literary critics and historians reassess one of the defining features of early modern England—the idea of "capital." The collection reevaluates the different aspects of the concept amidst the profound changes of the period.

CASTRATION
An Abbreviated History of Western Manhood

New in Paperback

Gary Taylor

"(In) this dense, scholarly yet thoroughly entertaining book Taylor posits that understanding what it means to be biologically unmanned is an excellent way to understand what it means to be a man. You don't need to be enthusiastic about this thesis—or even to be male—to find *Castration* terrific reading."

—Salon

CYBORG CITIZEN
Politics in the Posthuman Age

Chris Hables Gray

"...a supremely readable book, enlivened by weird science and slap-shot one-liners."

—Mark Dery, *Wired*

CYBERTYPES
Race, Ethnicity, and Identity on the Internet

Lisa Nakamura

"Nakamura argues that 'race happens' in cyberspace, and in her book a savvy racial analysis is what's on the menu... What we get from reading difference with Nakamura is a menu for change, not a recipe for more of the same."

—Donna J. Haraway

1 . 8 0 0 . 6 3 4 . 7 0 6 4

Online Access

This journal is available online in 2002

Institutional subscribers to the print version of this volume can enjoy online access to the same volume (and in many cases to the electronic archive) free of charge.

KEY BENEFITS

- Fully searchable database
- Active reference linking
- Easy access to full text
- Multi-format delivery options
- IP access control
- Cross journal searching
- Contents alerting service

Please connect to **www.tandf.co.uk/online.html** for further information.

SEND AN E-MAIL TO:

Online Customer Services Department – **online@tandf.co.uk**

Please contact Customer Services at either:

Taylor & Francis Ltd, Rankine Road, Basingstoke, Hants RG24 8PR, UK
Tel: +44 (0)1256 813002 **Fax:** +44 (0)1256 330245 **E-mail:** enquiry@tandf.co.uk **Website:** www.tandf.co.uk

Taylor & Francis Inc, 325 Chestnut Street, 8th Floor, Philadelphia, PA 19106, USA
Tel: +1 215 6258900 **Fax:** +1 215 6258914 **E-mail:** info@taylorandfrancis.com **Website:** www.taylorandfrancis.com